A CATCH OF ANTI-LETTERS

A
CATCH
OF
ANTI-
LETTERS

THOMAS MERTON

ROBERT LAX

Foreword by Brother Patrick Hart

Sheed & Ward

Cover and book design by Emil Antonucci

Illustrations by Thomas Merton

Library of Congress Cataloging-in-Publication Data

Merton, Thomas, 1915-1968.
    A catch of anti-letters / Thomas Merton, Robert
Lax ; foreword by Patrick Hart.
        p.   cm.
    Previously published: ©1978.
    ISBN 1-55612-712-X (alk. paper)
    1. Merton, Thomas, 1915-1968—Correspondence.
2. Lax, Robert—Correspondence. 3. Poets, American
—20th century—Correspondence.   I. Lax, Robert.
II. Title.
PS3525.E7174Z49   1994
818'.5409—dc20
    [B]   94-1262
                                                  CIP

Thomas Merton and Robert Lax first met when they were students at Columbia University in the late thirties and through their collaboration on a university magazine became close friends. Merton chronicled these years in his autobiography, *The Seven Storey Mountain*: "I thought I had something to be proud of when I became art-editor of *Jester* at the end of the year [1936]. Robert Lax was to be the editor and Ralph Toledano managing editor, and we got along well together. The next year *Jester* was well put together because of Toledano and well written because of Lax and sometimes popular with the masses because of me. When it was really funny, it was not popular at all. The only really funny issues were mostly the work of Lax and Bob Gibney, the fruit of ideas that came to them at four o'clock in the morning in their room on the top floor of Furnald Hall [pp. 155-156]."

Lax was a Jew and Merton not yet a Catholic (that was to come in 1938 for Merton and a decade later for Lax), and their friendship was to endure and grow throughout their lives. Both were poets and solitaries: Merton in a Trappist monastery and Lax, after much searching, on a Greek island. Merton describes Lax in another passage from his autobiography: ". . . he was a kind of combination of Hamlet and Elias. A potential prophet, but without rage. A king, but a Jew, too. A mind full of tremendous and subtle intuitions, and every day he found less and less to say about them, and resigned himself to being inarticulate. In his hesitations, though without embarrassment or nervousness at all, he would often curl his long legs all around a chair, in seven different ways, while he was trying to find a word with which to begin. He talked best sitting on the floor [p. 181]."

Mark Van Doren, who taught both Lax and Merton during their Columbia days, in his autobiography writes of them, recalling Merton as "merry and sober. . . . His blue eyes twinkled when he overheard a witty remark, or when he uttered one himself as often he did." Of Lax he said: "His chief secret, I have since decided, he could do nothing about. Least of all could he express it. Merton has described his long, lugubrious, humorous face, and has said of it that it seemed then to be the countenance of one who contemplated 'some incomprehensible woe.' The woe, I now believe, was that Lax could not state his bliss; his love of the world and all things, all persons in it [*The Autobiography of Mark Van Doren*, p. 212]."

Soon after graduation from Columbia Merton began teaching at St. Bonaventure's University in upstate New York, and Lax worked for a time at the *New Yorker*. Then they met Baroness Catherine de Hueck and felt attracted to her apostolate at Friendship House in Harlem. In a recently published book Catherine de Hueck Doherty reflected on Robert Lax and Thomas Merton and their concern for the plight of the poor and destitute huddled together in the ghetto of New York. Mrs. Doherty described Lax, "The Son of Israel" and his poetry-writing and floor-mopping activities at Friendship House. Of Merton, "The Man with the Deep-Seeing Eyes," the Baroness recalled that "my new friend wasn't very much different from Bob Lax. . . . It wasn't long before his friend [*Merton*] could mop a floor with the best of them, and even scrub it at times when necessary. He washed windows, looked after the clubs, led interesting discussions . . . [*Not Without Parables*, pp. 93–94]." But then, suddenly, in 1941, he decided to join the Trappists at the Abbey of Gethsemani in Kentucky.

Visits between these two men during Merton's twenty-seven years as a monk were not frequent, but they kept in close contact by letter. In the beginning there were serious exchanges of conventional letters. Lax and Merton were letter-writers in the best sense of the word, as their early correspondence bears witness. But the letters included in this volume are something else. They are anti-letters, friends in a playful mood exchanging thoughts on the world (including the "monastic world"), the Church and society at large, and must be read as such. Throwing grammar, syntax, and spelling to the winds, they write lightly—yet wisely—as two supremely free men, free "with the liberty of the children of God."

These anti-letters extend over a five-year period (1962–1967), commencing just as Lax was to begin his self-imposed exile on the Greek islands (Patmos and Mytilini, but mostly Kalymnos). The first exchange concerns a proposed Guggenheim Fellowship for which Lax had applied, and for which Merton was asked to write a letter of recommendation.

The correspondence proceeds with commentaries on the political scene as well as the local environment of the monastery, which Merton describes in a wild passage which bears quoting: "As for me my dear Charlot I sit in my hutch mimeographing forbidden books with the help of fifty-nine uncouth Albanian novices all highly irregular and dissipated ready for the most desperate acts. For the rest our situation here is too awful to be described, and I cease, falling at once into a stupid silence as is my habitual wont."

The letters are full of Columbia reminiscences of college friends and teachers. Among the Columbia professors mentioned in these exchanges are Mark Van Doren, professor of English and Comparative Literature who was to have such an impact on the lives of both Merton and Lax. Others included John Herman Randall, Lionel Trilling, Jacques Barzun, Irwin Edman, James Gutmann and Dwight Miner. Incidentally, it was Daniel Walsh, a professor of Philosophy at Columbia at this time who later told Merton about the Trappists and suggested a retreat at the monastery of Gethsemani.

The list of friends and classmates is more numerous beginning with Edward Rice ("Ed Rouse"), Merton's godfather and founder of *Jubilee* magazine; Robert Giroux, one of Merton's publishers; Ad Reinhardt, the abstract artist; Seymour Freedgood, editor of *Fortune*; Sing Ye, a Chinese classmate; John Slate who later became Merton's legal adviser; James Fitzsimmons, founder and editor of *Lugano Review;* Ralph de Toledano; Robert Gibney, who was to marry Nancy Flagg (both mentioned in *The Seven Storey Mountain*) and R. P. Smith, later to become a novelist. The letters immediately following the deaths of Ad Reinhardt and John Slate bring the volume to a close. Their passing was a sad event for both Lax and Merton. The latter commented: "Truly the bloom has faded."

Some examples of Lax's experimental concrete poetry are found in these anti-letters, such as the "song for daniel-rops" and "names and things." There also appear as graphic dividers some of Merton's Zen drawings, "flying signatures" as he called them, on which the friends comment frequently in the correspondence. (Some of these were later sold at Merton's instigation to set up a college scholarship fund for black students.) Several of Merton's poems are likewise included in this volume, such as "Night-Flowering Cactus" and "Seneca," which Merton sent to Lax in the letters, and Lax in turn commented on in subsequent letters. Finally, mention should be made here of the occasional references to some rather bizarre newspaper clippings exchanged between Merton and Lax in regard to "Miss Velma," a downtown Los Angeles evangelist. Merton used to send Lax newsphotos of her, with extracts from her sermons, in ever-changing scenes and get-ups, which are described in the letters.

A Catch of Anti-Letters was collected and edited, under this title, by Thomas Merton himself the year before his tragic death by accidental electrocution while attending a meeting of Asian monastic leaders in Bangkok. A selection of them appeared in *Voyages*, a Washington literary journal which has since ceased publication, but it was the hope of both Lax and Merton that they should be published in book form.

The first edition of *A Catch of Anti-Letters* appeared in 1978, thanks to the creative imagination of the late James F. Andrews, publisher of Sheed, Andrews & McMeel. It was well received by those discerning readers who recognized two great wits at their best. Since that edition was exhausted some years ago, and readers were asking for it again, we are grateful to Robert Heyer of Sheed & Ward for making it available at long last in a new paperback edition.

May the lives of all who venture into this unique correspondence be brightened by the humor and wisdom of these two solitary friends.

Abbey of Gethsemani / 31 January 1994

PART
ONE

I. ROBERT LAX

Here is a short note from the Insuls of Greichland to say that I have applied for a yo-ho-ho-erie from the Guggenhaus—that I have named you as my luckiest staretz and have given them right to ask you a frank appraisal of my staves.

Be frank, it is the only thing to be with the googenhows. (If you are not allowed to write, then leave it to Bro. Hilarion and if he not, to Brother Cellarer and if he not, Brother Barnabus, or anyone you like among the tigers.)

Here it is absolutely capital. The breezes, the landscapes & above all the people themselves, though Greek.

From here, toward spring, I think to Mt. Arthur—before that perhaps to Patras & même Mytilene. I am writing every minute of time—new poems, more poems.

Of money, as they say here, *tipota*. (One eats like the birds. One eats, in fact, birds.) One sings. One is contented.

Rice writes you were in and then out of the hospital. One hopes you are out now (for goods) and not in. That you are well, that you make handspring.

Write me here at this place when you can.

I am investigating the orthodoxes and they are very nice kids. (Of T-même they speak also very high and are quoting you in their pulpitries). Hesychasts are rare enough on the average street though some are certainly roosting in Mt. Arthurs.

Its almost, however, as though at the moment the RC's have more zowie and bam. (There ain't no bad girl, in the orthodox church, like Frarnce). All the orthos have got, when they're good, is clean spirits Now how are you going to go into a fight like that?

Anyways, write when you can.

Yrs,

c/o Eliot
4 St. Georgiou St.
Ekali, Athens

And so, my Dear Waldo,

It turns out that you are among the Greeks. This is clearly educational, especially as you refer to your Guggenhappy fellowspot, which is of an educational nature. And education is, I feel, what most interests the Googenspit. What then shall I tell them in my frank appraisals? Shall I not conceal how you hoot at the educations? Fifty dollars. Shall I not make hidden your scorn of the university? Fifty dollars. Shall I not bury in oblivion your contempt for the Greed's eppig Homware, Suffoelits, Europates, Askils? All you have contemned and spurned. Fifty dollars. Apart from that I will make light of Goggenball and fling reservation to the winds. How do you send me the sheets, the pencils, the carbons, the erasers and the microcards with which I am to inform of your spirits? Hath a high spirit, is indomitable, kicked over the traces at Columbia U., flouted Dean Hawkes, thumbed nose at Prexy Butler, a man of indomitable energies and corruscating Russian humors, burned all the books of the Greeks, smiled only at John O Hara.

No. This was only a joke: I will indite a long homework of praises for you bei dem Guggenfellow, a veritable epic in itself, substance and accident, category and isagoge, Porphyry and Isocrates shall spring into the gap with a pithy quip at the wrong instant, spoiling all, upsetting Guggy from his swivelchair. And you shall have millions wherever you go, principally in the Insels.

Let it suffice to say that the typewriter shall creak with your happy praises and the fellowships will be edified. Signed Staretz Nikodim.

I am going crazy trying to correct a Russian oddball history of mystics in Novgorod clearly a Red plot, fullup with sputniks and missiles named Tikhon. It is by a secret agent living in the cellars of the Vatican operating a telephone line with the Journal of the Moscow Patriarchate, telling everything Pope John had for breakfast ("rolls"). (Word comes back in Russky: "what *kind* of rolls?")

The last I hear of Greeks was in the travelogues of Henry Miller, the Coal House of Maritzpa. It was superb, enchanting, and I am still enchanted. I sigh for the Insels. Got another Greeks volumen here but can't read it for sorrows.

Many sorrows, but not for hospital. Was in and out of the hospital flushed with the most fearsome enemas, exasperated by nuns, weakened by medicals, infuriated by student nurses, woken in the middle of the night with hatpins, dieted with scornful trumpets which ran off shrieking to give all food to the harpies on some other floor, and instead of meals, enemas. I fling my glove in the face of all hospitals, never again to the hospitals or the hatpins.

General sorrows for Cubas, for the sadness of Werther, for the lamentations of the younger Schiller, for the lubugrities of the the elder Lessing for Laocoon, for the Tivoli fountains also, and for every work of plastic art. South America is in the doldrums, North America is for the lemons, we have a bird sitting on the capitol who sings a mournful threne, and within the capitol like so many blackbirds is Goldfinch Harvey the Bobwater with his companions baked in the less humble pie. When the pie is open the birds begin to sing, wasn't that a jolly portion to give to Guggenspin? So much for politics. The rest is in the poem which I have appended with bobby pins. There was an election and Bundridge was elected by the margin.

When I make the handspring I lose a hand. Otherwise plenty of vim.

Getting elderly, no more hat, no more head. Too dam much zowie in the Church if you ask me. Let's get back to the old restfulness, us and the orthos, less singing. More prayer of Jesus, more gazing at the navel, more kiss of God in the mossy wood.

I have sent to you under several separate blankets a host of forbidden books all written by me. To your New York agent, the sly Rice, in Jubilo.

And now who is this Eliot, you see I have come to the address. [*Lax was then staying with Alexander Eliot, art historian, novelist, and philosophic writer, at his home in Ekali, outside Athens.*]* You are staying with the very Eliot of cats. No, no. it has not come to this!

'I will make myself scarce as all the hesycat
And sleep in the sun with my Mt. Antic hat
I will make nine million the metanY
And turn into a MegaloskimY.

Tell them to go on preaching and not complaining.
  I wish you the best of the spring upon Mt Arthros.
  There is plenty doves someplace, not here.
    Farewell, a blessed Insel.
      Your Chum.
PS: For another fifty I will refrain from making known that you were Irwin edman's favorite pupil.

Also that you were frequently seen talking in corridors to James Guttman.

For my own part I am to apply pronto for a Guggenwald burse of ten million piastres for study in Rifraf, southeastern Turkey, whiles writing a polyglot series of volumens as follows:

1. Der Handschuh: twenty-five-thousand page novel about a lost handschuh.
2. Il Fileteo delle borghese: salacious spirituality for old ladies with holes in their heads.
3. Autour du Pepsi—Chatty French memoirs of my tour of the United States.
4. How I helped Lou Little Lick the Mustard Bowl. Memoirs of our days on the old five, or was it six? at Columbia Acad. Like when you rushed over tackle in a broad flam the last second before the demi tone which ruined Annapolapps.

IN FINE:

WILL HAROLD GUGGENBIRD HAND THE APPLE TO MINERVA? WATCH OUR SUNDAY SUPPLEMENT COPIOUS PICTURES.

III. THOMAS MERTON   *Dec. 3, 1962*

Has just gone off to the Guggenwhaps the total conclusions of my summation and reports. Let there be nothing secret among friends: I have filled out all the billets and schedules, the rockets, the whappets, the sheets, the warps and the lifestrips, with curricula, with analysis, with synthesis, with prognosis, with Te

---

Deums, with Magnificats and with all styles of happy auguries for commercial, supernatural and alchemical fruition of your mighty projects.

Let there be nothing secret among friends: here is what I have declared on oath, swearing violently upon Korans of every description:

Quoth: "This man is a great horse of fantastic power, and vivid eyesights, long hairy ears of acute sensitivity especially to Greek Isles. He runneth in the race with cunning, kicking the other horses off the track with a sly nudge of the fetlocks. He will assuredly win the Greek Derbies because of his intense eyesight and staying power. His moral character is beyond reproach, for he has seven haloes and five wings. With one more wing he will become a cherubim. It is rumored already in Mount Athos that this cherub, this New York Pegasus, is on the way with his vivid eyesight, for he has no fewer than twenty eyes, all of them very good.

Thus the monks have put away their whips and rolled out their ecumenical horoscope and decked the towers and onion domes with Greek and American flags arranged in a nifty pattern to spell in Greek letters: "G U G G E N H E I M".

In order to know how they get the H of Guggenheim into Greek letters it is necessary to give this man his fellowship and leave him alone to write verses among them Greeks. Do not bother him, just give him the fellowship and shut your traps, Misters. I threaten you with hideous reprisals from the Jubilee gang if you do not give him the fellowships he requires in order to remain a Greek."

With this and many another sly jest in five languages I have impressed upon their unskilled minds that you are sitting in Athens waiting for the check and they better get busy.

As for me my dear Charlot I sit in my hutch mimeographing forbidden books with the help of fifty-nine uncouth Albanian novices all highly irregular and dissipated ready for the most desperate acts. For the rest our situation here is too awful to be described, and I cease, falling at once into a stupid silence as is my habitual wont. Tell all the monks at Athos to light lamps in front of the ikons for me and pray I don't end up in the penal islands. Tell all the monks they should light up the vigil lights for peace. And turn on the new poems, man, turn on.

Yours ever Mittwoch,

———

Dear Mustwich:

What was my surprise and shock to go to the poso this am and find what do you think? Returned from Greeks my fond note of the three decembers a note inspired at the founts of Helicop with every sort of sly tune, penned with the viewless wings of popery, and with every Jesuitical trope and distinction. But what? Marked all over with Greek insults. "Agnostos" saith the foul postman, the bawd, the agnostic, the serf, the octopus eater. Agnottos Laxo, Agnostot Eliot, Agnotos S. Gerogiou, but I find on closer examination is that you are agnostos on B. Georgiou #4 but you are perhaps not yet agnostos at 7. Ah I pray that you do not be agnostos at seven, though as St. Paul well saith, looking around with a sweep at the Athenians, as he say in first Hebrews, "MEN I OBSERVE THAT EVERYBODY IN THIS JOINT IS AGNOSTOS." It was a great stir he created among the unknowns that spring morning in far away Athens long ago.

Thus I begin again and this time the letters are off to B Georgiou 7 and not 4 as was my churlish custom last month. Who knows how many superb poesies and other smuggled dainties have fallen foul of that chumless four? Go spit on four.

First then your poems my dear Borzoi are without doubt very fine poems I was surprised at the small thin lines running up and down the pages but on closer inspection I find them to be life in the raw. Really you have expressed with innuendos how people used to think when they had thoughts running through their minds. There is much zens in this. I like especially Theo you don't hate me do you Theo and the rest of it "a cause de ma folie." This poem I find very touching. This is the one I remember the most, but all the rest too. I guess it is no good giving such a good book to the critics but I don't think you ought to be keeping it such a secret either. For instance there is a man I told about it and he is half crazy mad for a copy and doesn't know where to turn. I guess I tell him write to Antonucci [*Emil Antonucci, New York artist and designer, publisher of Journeyman Books*]. Maybe also I better get some copies to give to friends in Argentina. Don't you go doing anything, I will just work on the channels, that is how I get books, through the channels, but this time with monies. The man who wants your book is a very smart fellow with Hutchins and if he once gets it you will be made known to seven or eight other people who are equally with Hutchins.

Henry Miller writes that he reads the Merton Reader every night for a nightcap and finds it most sober and ruminous. That is one of the goodies must have foundered on S. Georgiou 4, namely the Reader. You ever get the Reader? It is splendid and red with black on the back, name of the author in large titles, and full of materials by the author, the same is very pleased on this account. But if it was kicked down the front steps of St. Georgiou 4 then I am dismayed and in a dudgeon for fair. Let me know and I bring a copy personally always wanted to see Greece anyway.

Hope you got that old Guggenheim. I was in there pitching for your side.

Happy New Years. Stay at seven while my letters look for you. No more Georgiou four for me.

One of your personal correspondents

Dear Pertius:

Am I right in supposing you are still perched on that clump of
islands? What a perch, and if so, what a clump. Who would not
gladly emulate your wise choice of a villegiature or Greek spa?
Greek spas are always thought of as best. By any thinking man,
that is to say. But who today with even a lighted flashlight can
discover a thinking man? Agree with me, then, on your isles.

Here in our smashing madcap twenty century country all is
slipslop and upshot, coming out with moons and planets, down
with awful swats at the poors and the darkened. Truly a madcap
slipslop, you do well to avoid and to desist from thought of
return. Is it true the Guggenblat paid you not to return? If so I am
grateful and will go in pilgrimage to Googenspot and kneel on the
place where the decision was made.

Every century has had a hundred years more or less but this
one for iniquity already has two hundred though scarce half over.
It is a beastly aged century with long nails and unclipt comas
pretending to be the friend of man and withal devouring the race.
Do not give me the twenty first century, give me no more
centuries, give the centuries a rest. give history a surcease. give
historians all heart attacks. give politicians to have widows fast,
give up warmasters, yes, including Greeks. Give up I say the
warmasters and bombfats, leave alone the planners of
perturbations and exorientations. There is a very fast exorientation
predicted soon by Galen in his late book. It will be the slipslop
exorientation of Mars all over the planet. It will be a vast red soup
predicted though waveringly as to the minute by Hippocraps the
tame wizard of Gogs. Some think this has all stopped being
danger because there are now other jokes in the newspips, to wit
beakball and float-pop, or wish-polo, but I say that if all the beaks
were to break there would still be more to say about the
exorientations of the planet Mu. Yes, I have discovered with my
investigations of planetary minutiae that it has orbited Mu up and
down twenty five radii of the square of jet, and it will be revolving
e plus m to the 66 around Central Park next Tues. flat. So stay out
of the parks on that morning, stick to the isles, the isles are not
going to orbit in the same square roots. Less death rays around
the islands is my quip and motto for the day of birds.

Yes like I say my dear Pronto, since the late good Papst spoke of Pacems, everybody relaxed with a laugh and said thats it there can now be no more wars. whereas to the contrary my dear Pippit it is making faster and looser and bigger the more weapons every minute while talking through the back of the hand about negotiating.

Today is the new Papst, by name Pablo, a small clever Papst with greetings for all the people, and I sure hope he is clever enough to make them throw the weapons in the sea instead of on top each other as now planned. I think he got good will and agile footwork, which he will soon find himself to need, and even to need more than he already got. Prayer intention for the month of Julie: fast footwork of Papst to get twice as fast according to need. Within about one year his footwork got to be so fast that nobody any more see any feet at all, even with precise instruments.

In about thirty six hours I hope to send you many poems and ditties, as well as forbidden fruits of toil in radical magazines. I am for the most part very gay and hearty in spite of solid despairs, but I have discovered that despairs make jolly and all consolations and no despairs is for the dull monk to enjoy, but I do not say this out of vain hopes. Let all the glad abandon vain hopes and laugh until silly. There is little else to do. But plenty to laugh at.

by THOMAS MERTON

NIGHT-FLOWERING CACTUS

I know my time, which is obscure, silent and brief
For I am present without warning one night only.

When sun rises on the brass valleys I become serpent.

Though I show my true self only in the dark and to no man
(For I appear by day as serpent)
I belong neither to night nor day.

Sun and city never see my deep white bell
Or know my timeless moment of void:
There is no reply to my munificence.

When I come I lift my sudden Eucharist
Out of the earth's unfathomable joy
Clean and total I obey the world's body
I am intricate and whole, not art but wrought passion
Excellent deep pleasure of essential waters
Holiness of form and mineral mirth:

I am the extreme purity of virginal thirst.

I neither show my truth nor conceal it
My innocence is descried dimly
Only by divine gift
As a white cavern without explanation.

He who sees my purity
Dares not speak of it.
When I open once for all my impeccable bell
No one questions my silence:
The all-knowing bird of night flies out of my mouth.

Have you seen it? Then though my mirth has quickly ended
You live forever in its echo:
You will never be the same again.

from *The Collected Poems of Thomas Merton*
N.Y., New Directions pp.351-52

VI. ROBERT LAX   *July 27*

here is a bird i am send you
from Patmos

    this patmos is a splendid place. at first you wld think so, then
you would not, then you would think so again. the people are of
a very high quality; likewise the geography. what then if a crowd
of international sapristi shouters come up on their donkey-backs
with their cries of vois-donc and ooh (même) la la!?
    the people themselves are of the first cracks out of the box;
the landscape would drive poor sister winooka crazy with its
classical and religious references. if not in toledo, avila, or assisi,
then never have i seen such a pious landschaft.
    now to the heart of the matter: the goodies is arrived: the
scarves is all around their little throats; the mittens is been
removed only to give a cheer for uncle tim. now as to the goodies:
i like them all, each one, and especially my own particular
favorite, which is to say, night's cactus [*Merton's poem
"Night-Flowering Cactus"*]. this is some one hell of a poem, as i
think old r p smigh [*R. P. Smith: F*] might have say; and i am
write this minute to elgar rice he should print it, or if he print it
not, then i print it, on papyrs, or if i print it not, then perhaps

---

somebody else is already print it in the erich fromm's revue or the harriet muster's pome book.

all the poems he should print, every one; but for night-blooming cactoms, i will not take bach, i will not take dostoievskis.

now as to your tracts, dear Murtogs, i am in heartiest agreement with each of your tracts. do not be saying what you are saying, all you others, about the nigra; what you are saying, you, that is, for me is the only troothe. what they are saying is hawgworsh, every one; but what you are saying, you and jimmy baldwin are saying, these are the only truths.

this baldwin is a splendid fellow; you should have him to your monk-house; we try to get him from paris to come and shiver in eau vive, but him too smart; him smart as lightning; and like lightning, he is crazy for everybody: white & black.

also what you write for the unselfconscious is again the truth and looks out of place in the erich fromm's revue. what he says later for you is highly respectful, you will have to hand him that. he is no dumbhat like the others (erich up and erich of).

now let me say a word for ernesto cardenal, that he is a great personal favorite of mine; not only for his own splendid poems and translations, but that he inclus me in his fine collection & rejoice thereby not only myself but my sisters and friends. googenspiel is not inclus me. harriet muster is tell me lam. only ernesto cardenal, of all the collectors of poesie is inclus my ditties in his collection; and for this i am telling sister winooki to light him a candle swiftly & thus adieu.

The Patmos wines is easy to watch out for; not so the sicoudia of Crete. Watch out for this, yourself; a perilous object. If ever a monk should come from Crete with some of this, watch out for it, is all I say.

The man downstairs remarks to himself that I have beat long enough on his brain-pan. A truth. I conclude: the poems and musics are all of the highest order. Write more of these, and especially poems of the highest mystical nature; it is these that will shone forth when the smoke (if it ever does) shall clear away. Write, therefore, other highly contemplative poems.

I will write again. I will send you a picture of Patmos before I am chased.

Yrs,

"Eagle" Dunaway

[*Edwin "Eagle" Dunaway was a classmate and campus politician*]

VII. THOMAS MERTON

Dear Samos:

How come you all the time Samos? Glad about those Italian sheep and the head of the community. Some head, and some community. He no sheep by Cow. The Greek on the back if I can remember my Greeks, is trying to say "Where can anybody fly to from the race?" Then you turn over the picture and see the picture of this toothless Leader and you recognize the race. It makes you think. Not bad. Pretty smart poetry this Greek. Poet seems to have some kind of a dirty name, but you can forgive him a few things like that because of his verse. Where to fly from the genus? Where to take refuge from the species? In days like ours I think you can agree with me, my dear Patmos, that this is a genial and homely truth.

Me and Ad Reinhardt [F] have been carrying on correspondence by obscure telepathies and hidden calligraphic paintings of which I must send you one because I tell you Charlie I got ten million. I make the fastest calligraphic paintings in the world, twenty nine a second, zip zip zip all over Kentucky they fly in the air the doves bear them away to no galleries. My art is pure I tell you it is pure. Like I said got swarms of calligraphies the only thing wrong with them says Ad is they too small, only about a foot long, real calligraphies got to be so vast you can't get them out of the building.

What else does he say in his obscure and sly correspondence? He says he is going to chew you down for not being on the march. Says everybody ought to be on the march. I am mentally on the march. Mentally is best, it is pure and not exhausting. The march to which he refers is one which occurred some time ago in the national capital. It is positively the only march that has made any sense that I have heard about and that I have reason to regret not having been in. I am trying to figure out some way I can get

---

nationalized as a Negro as I am tired of belonging to the humiliating white race. One wants at times the comfort of belonging to a race that one can like and respect. This unfortunately seems to be something that has been concluded beforehand for everyone. Whence, says the Greek, shall one fly the species? John Howard Griffin did it with a pill but pills don't last. Meanwhile I take out my papers as a non-Saxon.

I send some manifestoes with the calligraphies because all I do and all I got is calligraphies and manifestoes, together with a peace prize which I won, but which I view out of the corner of the eye from a distance and with studied indifference. A Monsignor in Boston is going to pick it up for me at the back door of the organization, while I sit here and write more manifestoes, mostly humble ones.

As the days go by I mentally make another note that this is a further day in which Lax was smart to remain in Greece.

You tell Ad you was mentally on the march, you and the leader and the community and the Italians. I am marching up the wall along with Samos and the Japanese making all the time manifestoes. This is also mental. What matter? It is time to overlook the mentalities. In another envelope come the manifestoes. meanwhile I can't type because I am filled with rheums and schisms. In my spine it is rolling a busted disc. Medicine cries, "out with it" but prudence replies, "heavens no, let it roll. Better a spine with a disc in it than no back at all." Such are the mutterings of medicine in our time, and the quips of prudence. Was in the hospital again, all the same old things, cut, shot, bruised, battered, pasted, kneaded, heated, peeled, swept, chilled, fed, overfed, glutted, soaked, chopped and thrown back to the winter weeds of Nelson hills. Yes, and here I am with the weeds on and still a whole back, let us then give thanks to the Lord. Make a small march at Samos, for sympathy.

Yrs.

R. Higden

Listen, Hidgen,

i am always on the march. where have i been but on the
march. the banners is rippy & i can't remember what they say, but
i been marching all the time. (where did they go this time? i wish i
had of been there. my friends was there. my friends is always on
the march.)

did they get out of the white race? the black race? the human
race? flee from the race is what i say. i say it with the very last
tooth in me head.

i'm all right now. i never was on the march. reinhardt was
right. he was on the very first march they ever made. seymour
[*Freedgood: F*] said he was carried away with enthusiasm. where
was seymour when the march went by? i was never on a march.
helen levy was on one once. she made a placard that said dean
hawkes is a foo.

sing ye [*F*] (remember sing ye?) was on one once. his banner
said: up china. well, china's up now & i hope he's glad. but i ain't
never been on no march, and i ain't marching no wheres now.
almost wish i had a race i could belong to. i would rather be on a
race than on a march; that's where i'd rather be.

but now i'm all right again & i'm on the march. i've picked up
my things again & i'm marching, see? so where does it go? out of
the white race? out of the black race? down to the white race?
down to the black race? (toledano [*F*] was on the march: he
marched right into nixon's kitchen, they made him a doll called
itsy-bitsy-blue-eyes: that's the truth.)

I am sorry extremely about the choppings and cuttings; can
only advise as much recollection as foods (don't take no black man
pills, no pills at all) eat stuff like spinach if you can; all kinds field
greens; am living mostly on spinach & olive oil & yesterday
cleaned up 14 dogs in a fight. of the slipped (sic) disc, it is the very
seals of your wisdom that you told them no; leave the disc where it
is to scud about as it will. it is probably no slipped disc anyway. it
is only something they say when they haven't been using their
pliers in quite a long time. maybe it is a sacro-illium; i know an
exercise for the sacro-illium; but there must be no laughing in the
hall. you stand in a perfectly rigid position facing in any one
direction. you stretch your arms out to your sides, shoulder high;

then as though you was made of cement from the sacro-illiac down, not moving your hips or your feet: just the upper part of the whole assemblage: you turn slowly to the right & to the left: your arms still out at the side and turning with you: just five or six times all together. then you sit down. you are cured. (i learn this from old doctor travel, who, later (in the person of his daughter) was kennedy's & whereas once i could scarcely creep from pattern to pattern on the rug at the taft, i am now, almost constantly, on the go.)

that's what i'm on: the go, go, go. (cur stamus, cur non imus? pantote etsi) that last is greeks: means ever thusk.

old reinhardt is a splendid fellow and all but the king of the birds. his paintings is magnificent and works like dynamite when set down in any particular locale. they are all black paintings (get it?) black, black, black & can hardly help doing some good in the whole situation.

send me some calligraphies (i am in need of beauty); send me some manifestos (i am in need of instruction) and run (alas, hobble) to the chapel now & light me up a candle (i am in terrible needs of that, too).

i will also go on any marches you suggest or sign any manifestos you send me. but only the ones you are sending. i can't be signing manifestos that come in from every direction. ena programma is the only way.

send calligraphies right waya (some typewriter: hawaiian) right away. i am in need of beauty. i will be in mytilini till i get someplace else, and then i will tell you. i am stay in greece all the time in my hearts, but may have to go to italy and france (sometime around Christouyenna) on account of the exigencies. (my niece is in florence with an all-girls soccer team & i am like to see her there.)

must close now as the waters is come up about my ankles.

i am yrs.

D. Scott Decision

hey: i just read seneca. always surprises. always new things. beautiful poems, man, beautiful. write all the time more poems like that.

by THOMAS MERTON
SENECA

When the torch is taken
And the room is dark
The mute wife
Knowing Seneca's ways
Listens to night
To rumors
All around the house
While her wise
Lord promenades
Within his own temple
Master and censor
Overseeing
His own ways
With his philosophical sconce
Policing the streets
Of this secret Rome
While the wife
Silent as a sea
Policing nothing
Waits in darkness
For the Night Bird's
Inscrutable cry.

from *The Collected Poems of Thomas Merton* pp. 619–20.

Well then,

Today I receive your secrets about the march and your reminder of the manifestoes and calligraphies which I may or may not have sent. In order not to delay one minute now I am sending a generous supply of manifestoes and calligraphies to last you through the winter. The Greek winter is not reputed to be too severe and if you have to live on manifestoes, well, this has been done for centuries. So a shipload of manifestoes is on the way to Homer's towns.

What you say about the exercise is calculated to make me the laughing stock of the whole monastery but I will try anything once. It is rumored with many a heavy jest that I have been forbidden yogas and this is much to the liking of all the squares. How then shall I practice your exercise without making myself a byword? Yet I will try anything once and if the disc falls out they will all laugh on the other side of their faces.

Actually the remedy for the disc is to lie in bed trussed up in a traction reading the poems of George Herbert and lying on a hot water bottle red hot. This is no laughing stock because it is very prim, though I am secretly edging back to the yoga, lying in despair stretched out with my face flat on the desk instead of doing any writing. This is very salutary, while writing, on the other hand, calls forth groans and **makes** sick, but who said I was going to stop?

Let nobody deceive you, I am getting well. They will not come close to me with that instrument.

One of the manifestoes is about my having received a medal. This is not a sly way of forcing you to grant **me a** medal with *your* Pax, [*a one page poetry magazine published by Lax to which Merton contributed*] because there is another Pax, yes, there is a Pax in every **town** these days. The one that gave me a medal is a Massachusetts Pax, and this Sunday the 20th they hang a medal around the neck of a Monsignor up there who will sing them a song as from me. See the paper for the song. Why they give me a Pax medal I don't know, maybe it is because I am the only person who has failed to start a war of some sort in the last month. So when I say Pax medal be calm, it is already the other Pax, and by the time you get this I will have the medal and my pride.

Everybody else but me will be worn out from the banquet.

I will lie on the hot water bottle and tighten up the traction and read more of the poems of George Herbert, primmer than ever and more sly, fixing to start a war nobody has yet dreamed of.

What I said about the human race was serious and I am glad you took it serious. I am going to write to the Govt. about resigning from the human race. Or at least the white part, which is not by all accounts the most human.

For the rest I am marching no place.

Where is that book you were going to send? And where is that book I was going to send? The book I was going to send will take flight in November, it has a frightening cover which I like and is full of poems which you have seen. Not Seneca, though. I don't have the book yet. Nobody does.

Why don't you send a whole lot of your poems and novels in a bark to Mexico where there are people who will print them in a thing called El Corno Emplumado. I think they will do this, and they are printing seven calligraphies of mine one on top of the other just like they should be, in a series. This is very fine, because you can generally whistle yourself silly before you can find someone to print your calligraphies in a *series*. Their address is, Apartado 26546, Mexico DF. Always Apartado like all over South America, and the lady you write to is Margaret Randall de Mondragon. No relation to any Randalls [F] we know or any Dragons, but very nice, frank, friendly to poets, and exerting a good influence on all, though she neglects her Yoga lessons, she admits.

To these poets who are frank and simple I feel myself suddenly as a Father, but I hope not a Father Figure, and I better get those capital F's out of there quick. They got a very friendly magazine, it is almost like a neighborhood, of course a poetic neighborhood. Well, how's the neighborhood where *you* are? I notice that when you are typing they seem to *complain*. Is this *good*? Keep typing, and I'll keep typing. I spit on my disk, figuratively only of course, and if I get tired of typing I can always lie face down on the desk and relax, this is a new kind of Yoga nobody knows about and not verboten. It works for a cervical disc, anyway, but as for a sacroiliac for this my prudence has nothing to assert.

Hold up the side. Tell me if you got the pencils. Say Hello to

Georgiou, if I had more manifestoes I'd send them, but all I have now are thousands of useless manifestoes for monks, and as everyone knows, a manifesto is wasted on clergy, religious et al. As soon as you begin to declare anything they become deaf, and this is a remarkably useful aptitude to acquire.

Yrs.
Demosthenes
jul 27

X. ROBERT LAX

Hoy,
here i am again, yr friendly correspondent. i am read again the seneca poem & it is some poem. all yr poems, especially the ones like this, is great poems: not only the words but the music, not only the musics but the words. i am think right now (yet often before) you should write plenty poems like this; and even thus: as reinhardt makes now all the time the same black painting, make you also all the time the same dark poem; all the time, just that one poem: here a word, there a word, maybe a little different; only when you think it should be, until it gets to be tight as a sonnet: the music, the music always the same, here a word, there a word just a little different. this is my plan for your poetic career for the next little while; as soon as i get another, i will write you (if need be, later this afternoon).

now once more about the marches: i was on a march one time around the mayor's office (with placards, umbrellas and manifestos); the march was in favor of more dope for dope-fiends, but my sign only said: shame on city hall.

now again about the poems: write more poems and make more calligraphies: the poems help the calligraphies, the calligraphies help the poems; the poems and the calligraphies help the manifestos; you will see, you will see.

never try to say nothing in a poem(i say): only see it doesn't say nothing wrong. there ought to be a lot more poems (i say) only they shouldn't say so many wrong things. this must all be stopped. more poems, but not so many words and things like that.

well, that's all i got to say for now. that poem is some poem.

---

write more poems like that. send more poems right here. i am
always standing around for a new poem should come.

i had some more advice about the liniments too; but i think i
will wait and see how the first one went.

yrs,
Sam

XI. THOMAS MERTON   *Oct. 23, 1963*

Dear Jack:

It is true, no one can deny that you are the most friendly of
neighborhood correspondents you have treated the Seneca poem
with the most favorable condescension and interest, what you say
about writing both words and music is to me food for thought I
haven't got around to writing this one twenty times yet words and
music but I am thinking about it I recognize in your quip a deep
insights I say to myself Lax got the answers, Mitylene must be full
of answers, bright sky shines down the answers. You got the right
answers, I got to concede that, in Mytilene you have seen the light
you got all the right answers. I think this poem should get blacker
and blacker and blacker like Reinhardt's paintings, then everyone
will see the light, they will have to. Every man got one poem, and
when he stumbles on it he got to make it smaller and smaller and
blacker and blacker and then it will finally convince.

If you see any more lights and get any more plans you get
right down to the typewriter and never mind about the
complaining Greeks in the next room or downstairs or upstairs, but
you write me the plan, then I will take the same poem and make it
blacker and smaller. But I haven't done it yet, and I have been
tardy and negligent with the calligraphies but pretty soon there will
be a blizzard of calligraphies. Ad says all calligraphies have to be
large but in that case I am the father of the small calligraphy, and
the father of the microscopic calligraphy. Ernesto Cardenal's friend
the mad poet Cortes [*Nicaraguan poet*] whom I have translated (did
you see it yet) he writes smaller and smaller and always the same
poem and now it has to be read with microscopes he is almost the
best poet in the world.

You should be getting calligraphies wrapped up in

---

manifestoes, they are on the way by Greek boats. Greek boats are generally the best for manifestoes, and this one got plenty.

That march: when you had the sign about city hall you were right. You are right all the time. City hall ought to hear about your sign. I bet Ad Reinhardt didn't see you there with that sign, he was all absorbed in some black painting he was thinking about and he couldn't read your sign. It was the best sign at the whole march.

Ned O'Gorman was at the march, I know you know he was at the march though Ad Reinhardt was all wound up in some black painting and could not see him. I don't think Ad Reinhardt even saw the Lincoln Memorial at the march, he was immersed in some of his thoughts, he was in a brown study. That is as far as he can go when he is on the march. He gets no further than a kind of dusk in which he is sunk in a kind of black painting. Ned O'Gorman wrote about the march in a way that brought home to you how he had been present, and if Ad Reinhardt had only come out of his trance he would have seen him there. Also girls of Manhattanville were there but you didn't pay any attention and I didn't pay any attention and Reinhardt was lost in thought. Some march. Everybody in a trance. The Manhattanville girls eat well. They were plump girls in light dresses standing around wide awake. They had big signs with "LUNCH" written all over in large letters, that was what they had to say. Neither you nor I were bothering to look, we had the right dope, we knew what to think of City Hall. We were not thinking about lunch.

I don't need liniments, hate liniments, hate tractions, hate the hot water bustle, hate baths. Fie on liniment. Will eat no more cress, do you hear?

Well, never mind, you got the right idea about everything, and even if you tell me to drink the liniment I will do it. Now that you got the news shining right down from the sky of them isles I listen to everything you say, and I will get back to that poem or to another one just like it.

Took a huge picture of a Shaker house and maybe I will send it on a freighter to Jubilee.

devoted

Quincy.

I'll heave some more manifestoes in the mail right away.

Dear Captain Thurston:
Your letters is drift ashore and i am apprised now of all that is in them. (outside is bugles: another festa; every day for venezelos, another cheer.) you are keeping your disc on the bottles. you are stromped to your bed. this is very sad news. you are read the poems of george herbert. this is cheering. i have always had a great admiration for the works of herbert (and not only george but spencer); still you are in your beds; and from your bed you must not do the exercises because of laughing-stock); you must not do them as they are intended for another condition (i.e.: standing up) and i should suppose not hurting so much. perhaps it is one thing, sacroilliac, and the disc another. still, when you are standing up, you could try gently once. (i will look meantime in the satchel for other tricks.)

it is not alfred spencer i read at the moment, but j h randall, his novel about the works of aristotle. its title, just aristotle is misleading, as it speaks also of plato and the pre-socratics; but it is a highly instructive book and takes many a biff bam boom at st thomas of quinas. (am starting a tiny ockhamite college at the montauk end of mt athos, and will write you from there.) his advisements for taking a practical view and cheering for middle class virtues would make you want to join seymour fast on the boards of time life and fulcrum. (still he is a very smart fellow & not like some of the cats we had around there.)

now, to the manifestos. i attend the manifestos with impatience. my impatience has boiled over fifteen times in the past two days with the post office anyway, and now i am attending these with even more. you have been given a pax prize. the monsignor is wearing a pax prize. i can never be given a pax prize: I AM ALWAYS STARTING WARS. i will start a war with the post office right this minute until the manifesto and calligraphies have arrived. (you say it is not the only way, but for me it is the only way.)

i am happy about the pax prize. i knew you never started any wars, (you were always saying you started the hitler war, but i knew no). did you start the indonesia war? no, never. (i started the indonesia war, but i would never do it again.) on the contrary, you are, if anything, *against* war. do the pax people realize that?

i am not talking about that other pax, i am talking about the massachusetts pax. that other pax will give you a shiny, invisible prize: it is called the far-and-away-the best-contributor prize, and this you can wear all your life. (pretty soon we will put out a greek edition of pax: a *fie on war* issue, while talking about nothing but birds.)

the book, the one in november, i look forward to with impatience. it is best you sent me a letter first: where are you? then i will tell you; then you will send it. for i will leave here soon for athens; then from athens to corinth? calchis? kalamata? (does any of them sound good?) still even mytilini is all right, for they are smart in the poste restante; and athens, too all right (poste restante, athens 133)—the 133, although underlined is nice, but not important; but no st georgiou, get it? no st georgiou. for writing, write me here to mytilini, then i will write you when i have some new address.

the book, the one i'll send you: maybe it is this: the last half of the first book and the first half of the second. why so crazy (you may well ask)? it is because that is all the copies i have (right now) as a man named kimon friar is sitting on one in athens. he will not sit on it long. i do not know him from rairf nomik, but know he will not sit on it long.

& i will send some poems to mrs. dragon (all about she should stand on her head and breathe deep); she must be some woman if happy to run calligraphies in a series.

what poems will i send her: the kind that go zoom-zoom-zoom? or the kind that go yesterday-it-seems-to-me-i-forgot-where-i-put-my-hat? etc. well, i will wait till the spurs of the moment and send her instead a picture of my aunt.

am learning greek now all the time with grammars & accents: ancient greek, modern greek, philokalia greek; i can order carrot-greens in any language.

(it is alright now about the typing. i am living in what seems to be a swiss hospital on a tiny elevation in mytilini. the other patients stumble in at three in the morning, dropping their paper hats in the halls; but the rest of the time it is silent and sombre as fort knox.)

Yrs,
Lycourges

Dear Arthur;

yrs is arrived, and i am delighted with the following news: that you are in favor of small black poems, small black calligraphies, small black musical compositions and immobile small black dances.

i, too, am in favor of all of these, and have of recent months become so generally small & black myself that it is useless for me to apply for abrogation from the whites. how come you want to get out of the race (they would snigger) you was never in it. you was never in it. you're not so white yourself (is all i could ever reply) you're not so white yourself, you red baboons.

i have sent you (with birds) the first pt of the second volume of the book i am always writing, the first vol i will send you later when i can get it (but it is nothing at all to be restless about); this second volum too, is a flock of confusions, but you will see, you will see.

now i must needs pack up and go to europe (as it seems): my niece is there for Christmas & i will go & ride with her from italy to frarnce & back again; (this is good, she is a splendid niece) then i shld be back in mytilini again in early march.

best place for mail i think is mytilini: i will keep telling them where i am, what to hold and what to send (all these travel plans keep me awake all night like a very carthusian).

anyway, it is coming here the dark umbraceous winter (not today, today is fine); all night it will rain on the olive trees and in the morning the cobbled streets are up to your knees in mud. my pleasure these days (to change it all) is the admiration of greek grammar; i haven't learned much yet, but only to see the way it is laid out hath left me in a state of dazzlement. the entire world should be as neatly labeled as these greek adverbs. as well, the interjections. the laughing interjection hath but one example ááá. whereas the thaumastic hath both:á (another a) and ó.

it is bright outside but cloudy in here. i must find my shoes again and pack my things. fie on the liniments and tractions, as well on the cresses. yr. letter gave me great pleasure. i am glad if you think we are on the right track. this book i am sending will not make you think so, but never mind the book. write again if you

can; even poste restante, athens; i shld be there by nov 12 & will
tell them where i am.

yrs,
Albert

XIV. THOMAS MERTON

Dear Vince:

Here is your uncle pangloss again writing hard from Moose
Holler, where the Bears whoop and the bobcats scramble up and
down the stockade. And you? I have a plan for correspondences.
This one will be sent real sneaky into Athens 113, even though it is
immaterial I always put in the 113 just to be safe. I never going to
forget what happened with that Hagiou Georgiou. The book I will
send when you have informed by whales what corner of Corfu you
are part of. The book has come one copy. I mean my book, wait a
minute about your book. It has a frightening cover but inside is
tame and meek, though sometimes mutters in an undertone about
the state of our times.

Now you are the master of the undertone. It is now your
books that I discuss. Where is your books? I look around at the
mountain of existentialism with which I am at all times surrounded
and I do not find your books. Never mind, they are both, the large
and the small, printed with letters of gold on my memories. My
impression of your book is that it has got to be all or nothing with
the publisher. That is to say you got to convince the publisher by
your firmness that it is all or nothing,the truth being that it is not
otherwise even for one minute. Like they can't take two picas of
black white black white and leave the rest. Its got to be all or
nothing and by all I mean the whole book, the whole book is one
poem, and I think it is to modern poetry as is Ad Reinhardt the
Sufi to modern painting. It is just like Ad Reinhardt and Ad
Reinhardt is just like it, and the book is so good that the typewriter
ribbon gets darker with enthusiasm. You are right about small
black poems and not resigning from the race (who has to? who
bothers to resign?)

Let us for the moment set aside the reader of your book who

will not play all or nothing and will not attend to every bit of black white etc. For him there is no nothing, there is nothing there, set him aside, resign from his race, stop the train and let him off. And keep on with the black white, every pica is necessary. It is good sometimes that the bird wants to fly over the valley, but the constant black white that is like Reinhardt, and underneath this book is the real poem which is not to be spoken, the guys who do not go all the way to the real poem better stop the train and get off, and they already have, they were never on the train in the first place.

If anybody comes up to you and say what does it mean what is it for black white stop the train and drop him off or remind him he is not on the train. These poems are the only ones really easy to understand that have every been written, and other poems that seem easy are a big fraud, taking away the customer's money for an illusion, whereas your poems are very easy to understand they mean exactly what they say, black white, blackblackblack, etc, what is simpler than that, what the idiots want anyway, you should draw them a damn blueprint of blackblackblack? Already you see the mystifications involved in such a program my dear Buster. You are the only poet today who is not imposing in the public a very great hoax. However the great question of the public that pays only for a good hoax and nothing else, this I leave to other considerations at another time and by somebody other than myself.

As for your thaumastics you are plenty smart to take up thaumastics. Me too. Thaumazo thaumazeis, etc. you can't fool me. Thaumazo ta poemata sou. Ha Ha. Don't got the right accents on this typewriter but got plenty accents, watch: é é é, èè, ééé, èè, àààà.

àààà, éé, àààà, éé, áááá çè çè caca caca (for the censors a little caca, otherwise they would be duped and hoaxed.) u u, uu, uuü. cu cu, cu cu, cocu, cocu (for the censors a little cocu, how they ever going to do any business if there is no cocu in the manuscript?)
éo éo éo.
zä zqä zaâ
rô rô hô hô hô hô/
zaaaaaaaaaaaaa -á
This is just a few samples of my thaumastic typewriter.
Now for a genuine carol:

O and A and A and O
Cum cantibus in Choro
Let the merry organ go
Benedicamus Domino
Oooooooooooooooooôl.
Well, when I get another copy of my vast purposeless elegies I will
send to wherever you say in Corfu or among the Slavs or even
among the francs. Back to the francs? I have resigned from the
francs.

Be as thaumastic as you please
All around the Isles of Greece
Go your way and go your way
On that thaumastic holiday.
Explicit poems.

XV. ROBERT LAX

Nov. 27
Athens 133

Dear Doctor Moosehunter,
 Your letter with its many ingenious thaumistics certainly came
to me at a good moment. I am in agreement with all you say,
because all you say about the poems is good.
 1) All or nothing. That is good.
 2) Hidden poem under the poems. That is good.
 3) Black & white is good, is good.
 I think the black & whites or, even if there is no hidden poem,
even if the birds in the valleys must sit by themselves. If black &
white's OK, is up & down OK? Is in & out OK? (Sometimes I don't
know at all, but I feel OK about black & white)—maybe not black
on black, but black & white OK.
 About the others: the life and hopes of Muriel Spingarn—these
I can take or leave alone. It is all right, I guess, we can print 'em;
but I can take them or leave them alone.
 4) Let the reader get off the train—that is good. (Ho Ho. I can
see him now getting off the train—Ho Ho for the reader.) Here's
your hat with its over-hat, here's your collapsible umbrella. (It's a
rain train, Jack, so you better get off.) Some reader.

5) Ca ca for the censor. That is good. However that is all the ca ca there is. Let not the true reader be offended, let us see to that. (In the quiet of your house you can tell where & when the reader will be offended & of this you must be quick to let me know, cut it out of the ms, I say, cut it out.)

Let me see; that is all. Your elegies are of an enchanting beauty; your lyrics & thaumastics most heartening; your typewriter's accents are of the finest.

As to your book (with its quiet insides) I await it with impatience modified only by the complexity of my addresses. If you have already sent it to Athens 133 or Mytilini, there is nothing to fear. The entire police force in Mytilini is waiting. But if you have not sent it, I would say wait till Spring (early March) when I hope I return. (Else, if you think good, you could send to Paris.)

Wait & I will tell you when I come to Mytilini. As to the other Bk, Bk 1, the second I am sending, it is coming by way of idiorhythmic whale; irresponsible, but only costs 5 drachmas & should be there by Jan. 15 or Mars. or April. When it comes, I hope you will read as much as you can straight through—that is all I hope (& mark out the parts the printer should leave alone). Emil is dancing in the streets right now to make enough money to print this book, but I don't want to print no book that shouldn't be printed.

Happy Christmas now, is all I hope. I'll send this letter off so it will get there. No poems in this letter. In next letter, maybe tomorrow. I wrote some poems on a rock in Aegina.

Yrs,
Sam

XVI. THOMAS MERTON   *Mar. 5, 1964*

Dear Zmano.

First of all your prose is again from Greeks which alerts me to the fact that you have not budged an inch. Bravo. Lest you budge again, more bravo.

Now in addition to this you send me the spots and the hots of Rimini [*Lax had sent Merton a published list of pensiones in Rimini*] and I have studied each one with a conclusive inspection final and thorough and I am still in the airs as to whether I shall take up my sojourn at the Soggiorno Sport (most fitting since I am a sport) or at the Sombrero (since I have no hat) but maybe it is after all to be the Swinger, though for my own part I prefer the Locanda del Lup, not to mention the Sogno d'estate since it is now inverno. Oh bello sogno!

As to the Stadt Koeln I sneer and upon the TV I groan with abhorrence. These are for German sailors only. To the Tuberosa I will not go, since I know full well what a character of establishment is this, you cannot fool me, I can tell a bordello from a great distance even two thousand miles. Tuberosa indeed. Yeah, and Ilde too. Your can't fool me with Ilde. Nor with Mimosa, nor with Ondina, still less with Tres Jolie. That place Rimini ought to be investigated. Finally Quiete (La) is most abominable of all for I know what kind of quiete they got in their La. It is quiete with dopes and dusts, with needles and pokes, with pipes and flicks, with sly nods and hums, with Chinese poppies and Rimini cigarettes of a kind that need to be investigated more than even the Villa Apis (and THAT'S ANOTHER ONE).

Don't move from where you are. I will see that the Polognese and Beau Rivage are locked up both singly and doubly. You are safer where you are. Innocent names of Pensiones, my dear Bardo, but never a pensiere in the pensione, it is all license and flouncing up and down. How do you like this one: Holliwood, yes, Holliwood. How do you like that? They think that they can put one over on us with an "i" in Holliwood. O the beasts! I know what they got in their Holliwood: flouncings. Dusts. Grenadine syrups. Cocacolas.

You have made me muse, you understand. You have brought about a flood of these surmises and poetic trains of thought. But all is not poesy in my strange life of sadness, facts, events, proses, newspops, flashbacks, inopportune memories, corrections, restatements, retractions, mulling over the weekend, saying what was never said, hearing what was never meant to be understood. One of the saddest facts of my factual existence is that I am in perpetual trouble with the hoodwinks and the curials, with the bonzes and scrabs, with the imperial tomes and the forthwith communicado from the Vaste Curie. It comes to me with tubes from the eternal city a constant flood of reprehension and surveillance and I am under the wraps, forced into the corners, smoked out of my den, smoked back into the wrong dam den, never know where I am next, got no more category, lost identity, forsook my crazy number whatever it was, got three names all of which false, forget who was my uncle Hardold, forgot Douglaston again. I am more reproved now that I was in Douglaston and Great Necks. I have a hole in my muscle. I have a chunk out of my back. I have a place inside my lip. I have an empty stomach. I wish for the fried egg but in vain. I am off to Japan but only in the imagination. I am haled before all the councils with a red pencil. I am accused in the Milanese. The sports in the Soggiorno have given up awaiting my arrival. I have no more advents. I am crushed under the rug.

About your poems my dear Mappo I find myself in the position of being sorely inhibited by a trance. When I look at so many long small poems and say to myself that I am to get busy and edit, I am overcome with a faintness and with a swound. The luster comes and goes in my eye quickety quick and then the head goes out with a swump and I am smack off in the moon or someplace doing another thing of vast triviality. All the time it is the same swound when I got to do anything artistic except calligraphies. With calligraphies on the other hand it is always a great storm of creative action and the calligraphies pile ten miles high and I am buried and smother under the dam calligraphies there is so much action and creation. This is what they must have heard for them to elect me to the Presidency at old Soggiorno, and to the Secretaryship of Villa Driade. Yeah, I know what kind of place, but I accept anyway. And I am also Judge in Chief down at Stella Alpina.

Returning to your poems. I find myself approached by a small insidious lethargy when the sense of responsibility comes zooming down upon me from this volume, I fight off responsibilities tooth and nail, but maybe when I get more to eat, fried egg for inst, I will myself swoop into the air, unbend the wing, unfold the coleopter, and smick smack right and left attacking old duty with a vim. This is no reproach to you for your poems or for the magnitude of the volume or the overwhelming mass of the responsibility. Must up and meet the responsibility, I moan in my misty threnes and so back to the calligraphies, the volumes of piety, the tussles with censor of losing battle for peace on earth among the sanes, the new flying poems, the old Zen mystics, and the etc of every morning or afternoon.

———

Be patient with me yet a while and I will fling the lethargies far and wide and become worthy of your trust, I will become worthy of your trust, I will shoulder the truss and become warden of the responsibility, I will undertake the commitment, I will boot out the lethargies in their swarms, I will storm Random House with carrier pigeons.

Maybe it will come out like this. Antonucci print maybe say some calligraphies of me and some poems of you, I pile up million calligraphies and select poems then we all see what next, and then I hide again and the ill bird swoop down some more from the Curial Cafeterias where I am reproved in the Generalizia. After all this the crown, the crown, the nimbus, the aureole, the gladium, the scutum et bellum, the gloriosa gesta, the victoria. Where Morse is thy victoria? Doot doot doot dashdash.

Farewell, be prudent, be joyful, up the geraniums.

XVII. ROBERT LAX
March 13
P Restante
Kos

My dearest Zwow,

it is good back here. wow wow wow to be in europe was just like being in souf ohio: same old juke box, same old pin-ball, same old absolutely nothing to 'do. the villa tendresse indeed: out of the box i'd get to choose the pension t-v. (any news of the bums? what did you say? i said: any news of the bums?)

now as to the calligraphies: wow! (another type wow); i am like all the calligraphies, all, all, and especially the one with my name on it: it is some calligraphy: zaup! do not stand in your own way when it comes to making calligraphies: do thousands; they are all great calligraphies.

it is cold here, let me admit, at the pensione clepsydra; and the willys comes up from the floors; but it is greece and that is more than you can say for anyplace else, even turkey (i will come to turkey; a lot of people maligning the turks and moslems, but let us reconsider their position; let us reconsider it at some other time). i forget to mention the letter to poets which is arrive this morning. it is wow wow wow: just what the poets is needing: just what i felt i was coming to see in the graces of yesterday afternoon: that this is what poems is all about, this is what every poet should know. (perhaps you would have a monk friend send me one copy two for some of my friends poets.)

but now as to the troubles, i am stricken about the troubles: especially the chunks from the back and the hole in the muscle: no chunks and holes: fight them back every time when they try to get near with their clippers: let them approach only if they bring, to say the least, fried eggs. no, no, better the hotel sport; better the pensione trivia. consent to no therapies rougher than the sitzbad: sitzbad cures all ills. (not so, not so the hotel clyster; stay away from the hotel clyster too.)

as to that with the head of the filing department: it is all a part of the regular scene (they will paint themselves into a corner, you will see) it is all a preparation for the crowns and aureole, scutum and bellum, pensione gloriosa. (remember how we hailed the opportunity of reading our works to the court in bradford? it is all very much the same) as to uncle Hardolt in douglaston: i hear he is Clement the 21st but that is not for a while yet.

the bk: i think the thing is, let it sit there. Or send it off to fort tacoma. i don't want it around the house unless it's got a suit on. (no more bumbly old overcoat.) we got other kids in the house.

yrs,
Sam

XVIII. ROBERT LAX *May 1*
kalymnos

dear doctor,

here it is good friday among the orthodox (i have just again seen old pater basilis) the following questions are in my mind: how do we know we're right and they're wrong? how do we know that maybe we're both right? how do we know that they're not right and us wrong?

(why do we think we shouldn't give up our special claims and just become one church among the orthodox?) (is that what's going on?) at all?

here in kalymnos, anyway, not much clarity; but i like it.

(other kind clarity; more marseille than la salette.)
write me something (anything) mytilini.

L

PS: nothing seems much better (on this side) except it all seems more real (like the good are good, the bad are bad); no giggling, no self-consciousness, like we got plenty, and the anglicans got worse. (it's taken me two years of sitting around to even notice this much.)

XIX. THOMAS MERTON   *May 8, 1964*

My Dear Ludolf.

That is the way. Sooner or later we start it. Who is right, we say, who is wrong, who has the reason, who has the unreason, to whom the recht and to which the tort? Let me go back in history: Mussolini ha siempre ragione. The more anyone cried about the errors the more he bellowed back about the ragione. Is it human to err? It is alas more human to have ragione. It is however divine to have ragione all the time, especially when one is only a politician.

Thus having laid down no foundations whatever for a discussion, I proceed with the question: who is right?

My dear Ludolf, without putting on the frock coats of Bouvard and Pecuchet, and without either removing, or not removing, the pince nez of the nineteenth century agnostic, while at the same time affirming "yes" and roaring "no" I would like to point out who has the ragione and who has the errore. It is Mussolini that has the ragione. When? Sempre. Or siempre.

Ragione is everlasting upon the frock coat of Bouvard and Pecuchet and the pince nez of Bouvard pinches the nose of Pecuchet.

Thus it is clear that Bouvard has ragione and Pecuchet has the pince nez.

Or to be precise it is Bouvard that pinches and Pecuchet that sneezes. Which after all is the unrecht in this old squabble? The answer then my dear Imbroglio is that the Church has the ragione and the devil has the errore. Now you say which is the Church? Must we therefore begin again?

Once more from a different angle.

The tree is known by its fruits. Let us now turn to some other topic.

And now from the angle of faith. Between us and them is no difference of faith, is no difference. Is not a whistle of a significant difference, that about the Filioque was dreamed up by Germans and it is something got to be undreamed by the same Germans. It is none of my business.

Difference between us and them is politics, chum. Is a historical question of politics which neither you nor I nor that monk you spoke of got any time to bother with. Let the politicians figure it out. Let the Vatican figure it out. Let the fanna or the sublime porte or whatever you call it figure the whole thing out. For us what we got to do is lay off the cavilling and each in his own way be a whole Christian. It happens that you and me are in the Church of Rome with our customs, etc etc and our customs etc. You know what I mean. And they are there with their set of customs etc etc etc you know that I mean you seen them closer. OK should we mess up another big stew of customs when the whole thing likely to blow up anyway? My hunch is that one day we all get together with those guys in the concentration camps and discover there wasn't any disagreement, we are all the same corpses.

Right now we are a big pickle jar with everyone stirring up the thoughts, this one ecumenical and that one who knows what? And echo gives back who knows what? Who is to answer when echo gives it back so unclear?

For instance they come up to me and seize me by the lapels and by the pince nez and scream at me about this Soloviev. Did they ever seize you by the lapels etc and scream at you about Soloviev? The Russian Newman. Newman also was the English Soloviev. Everybody screams like mad about Soloviev and nobody is very sure about what is all the screaming. At one point Soloviev was Catholic Romish and at another point he come to die and called in the Ruskies. Hence they grab you by the lapels, etc. etc.

Now to my mind my dear Ludolf all this is wearing out the lapels without a purpose.

I think there are too many conferences and much in the press, as the bard says, much ado about numquam.

It is to my mind that in the Holy Ghost and in Christ we are one and as for the visibility it is now obscure.

I do not wish to explain to the guys how it is we are one because I don't know.

Each one has to sit in his hutch and do his best,

When then comes up to me a Baptist and diffidently says this or that I reply: "stay in your baptisms."

Whole groups of people I tell "Stay put, what for you cross the fence?"

What fence?

Why do you have to stick your dumb face in the Holy Office? (Not you, I just take this on title of an example.)

Wait until the Holy Office is removed and the fence will drop automatically. Who is to remove the Holy O-f-f-i-c-e??? That is for you not to figure out. You think the Holy Ghost don't know about the Holy Office? Well?

I was reading a guy called Rozanov who says Christians are all the time sad. This is true.

Except for the false optimism of Christians who rush about with the cheers of T. de Chardin on their pennant. This is thought to be a winning team, but like I say to every man his own hutch and sit quiet until the weather clears.

I guess the next best thing is to send goodies in the mail, so they come goodies to Mytilene. I don't know what to write to your monk. What is he going to do with India?

Stop and go to sing praises.

Yrs.

XX. THOMAS MERTON   *May 11, 1964*

Ho Lexos

There is a great hollow banging on the building and I suppose apes have come and would enter through the wall but this is nothing: they have so many already entered by the windows. Who is ashamed of apes? Not I.

What prompts me to resort once again to typescraps is that in my last epistle when the smoke had cleared and the reports was gone to Greece I clean forgot I had failed to save up the news pearls which I had treasured for you from many weeks. It is

---

essential that you keep up with the news because if you remain in Greek isles much longer and I hope you will, there is every promise that you will become impervious to events, and this is not for a boy of our century to become. Who shall be impervious when there is a Red in every drugstore putting brainwash pills in the cocacolas?

Now this news that I send is all of the highest import and comes from reputable dailies in Mexique, Madras, Singapore, Jodphur or Hodjpur, and many other points of meditation but chiefest of all Mexico. In case you are not impressed by these somewhat grey impresarios you must realize first of all that there is a revolt everywhere. First in the ladies jail is a revolt because the dope trade was interfered with and there was no water. I can imagine the ladies and their sly quips, when it is said that they are without shoes the shoes having been thrown at the polizei and there is much trampling garbage which was made for the occasion by means of their riot. Thus is asserted: "They cried out for lack of water the recluses." For lack, that is to say for failure of the waters or from deprivation, and it adds they did this "mediating through dirtymaking cries of protest, the destruction of meubles or meublas, (what meublas?) glasses and maybe pillows or mattresses and casting upon the ground or rather flinging down the nourishments which they had received from the polizei which we see on display to the both side of the imago." The signal: says a subheading: "The signal: *throw the soup!*" "At twelve o'clock when the service of the reclusory produced the dinner the ladies at this same moment cast it down upon the floor. This, as it appears, was the signal." . . . "The closers of the jail were not able to control the ensuing confusion. They appealed to grenadiers who appeased the souls of the disgusted ladies."

Later we find Fernando Garcia Francis the commandant of the reclusory reunited with the ladies in the patio and vociferating this question; in the midst of the scandal: "What is the cause of this disorder?" "The reply was not long in coming. The exalted recluses gave vent to their observations."

Passing on to other revolts, we have in Rochester NY a secretary who renounces because her chief prohibited to her to smoke the pipe. I draw your attention to the distinguished matrimonio which, like all of the same, presents an appearance of seriousness and even ill will. But what do you think of the apprehension of Presumed Robbers? It is the little rascal on the left that gave away the other two. I ask you to imagine his future.

When you have suitably meditated upon these woes of our time I ask you to make known far and wide to all Hellas the advantages of liberation.

I struggle with the shade of Plato. Was he or wasn't he for the likes of us? After many years of hesitation I am to suppose that Plato was on the right ball only if in the wrong game.

I am not struggling with the shade of Aristotles.

I have written a small leather book in secret language about Gandhi.

Be well, take the vitamin, snort the rich soups, watch out for the Greek milks.

Here come the Priors, stuff all the stuff in the letters quick. Ooops.

XXI. ROBERT LAX *poste restante*
mytilini
5th may

dear friends in the outer circle of the john stuart mill society:

i address you once again in my new listless style feeling it to be the most appropriate to our times, filled as they are with *utterly meaningless* bustle. bustles says the machine: filled as they are with utterly meaningless bustles.

XXII. ROBERT LAX

Dear Harvey,

i am here again at the machine, a prisoner of sorts in room 13 of the hotel rex. this hotel rex is a former crazy bin i believe, and they will never get the formaldehydes off the floor.

i am in receipt of all your notices, all joggling around at this moment in my heart and head.

stay in the hutch, says the one. i will stay in the hutch. another says carol harris, is smoke a cigar. and here is in mexique the reluctant bride; no, it is carol harris with a new cigar. she repeats her former accusation: if such is the price one must pay to defend one's proper convictions, then my determination is indeed correct. hurray for senorita Schmahl. i have read as well of the soup on the floor incidents, and the courageous words of Fernando Garcia Francis, the commandant of the reclusory. i am back again in room 13 of the hotel rex. the signal is once again: tirar la sopa.

i will stay in the hutch. their priests are like our monks. i don't know what their monks are like, the only word for nun is kaligria (nice old lady). but nobody means it. their nuns are really like the eumenides. sister savonarola: sister torquemada; sister hecate; sister styx. (never a little flower of anything.) there used to be one at la salette they called *la petite chose*, but she wouldn't last a minute in these insuls.

let me return to the priests and say that while they sometimes laugh, they never giggle; that while they are often well fed, they are seldom apoplectic; and that none has ever been seen in a checkered golf cap.

as to their relationship to the congregation, it seems to be hands in gloves. which the hand and which glove, it is hard from the distance i stand at to appraise; but anyway there is no great abyss or chasm, as it were between eternity and man.

i will stay in the hutch. i don't want any hands in any gloves. let them stay where they are. let me (for a minute) stay right where i am (room 13 of the hotel rex). i will figure things out for myself.

i do not mean this (for a minute) to sound rebellious, i am on my hands and knees night and day looking for a hutch to stand in. but there is no hutches on the floor. (only formaldehyde.) and father basilakis has gone to india.

i don't know if he has gone to india. I don't know what the indians will make of him (chutney) or what he will make of them. maybe he only likes orthodox hermits. and maybe he only knows one of them. (i don't really think you have to write him, and i don't know what you'd say; but i can tell you this: he's prepared to wait for 300 years till you do.)

i get a letter from gibney [F]. he has invented a new soap, *skunk*, for the ageing man: don't wait for nature to make you offensive. i get a letter from the japanese gardens at jubilee. i will stay in the hutch till it falls on my head.

on one of the islands i seen a small boy with a long sweater down to his ankles on which was embossed the word: nacoms [*a "secret" society at Columbia to which Merton had onced belonged*].

(i have no other news)

yrs,

and yes, oh yes: i am in receipt of every manifesto: of the monk in the diaspora, and suggestions for the amelioration of the rule: i am in accord with every word (the slyer the thrush the greater the accord) also (and perhaps most of all) the solitary life, a beautiful book i would like to have tatooed on me. and it comes to me the following thought, perhaps you could have your company send me to mitilini some more copies, a few, of this book, the solitary life, i should send to my friends who are looking around for a life of some kind, and perhaps this is it.

must close now, as here come the chamber-haunts.

yrs.,

XXIII. ROBERT LAX   *kalymnos poste restante july 4th (shut up)*

Hoy Captain Belsford,

one is in kalymnos. it is better here. the books are arrived. i thank you and every monk among you for the books. i will send them to lonely types through the world commending them on their solitary living. is another book name of hoopsaboy i am sending to the sybarites, thus all are contented with their lots.

i, for my part, am content with the present situation: two upstairs rooms of light blue white-washed surroundings in a house on this hill in kalymnos. downstairs an old lady stumbles gathering eggs. this is a village full of wise old men is got no wool on their eyes. i will send you examples of their wisdom in a following letter.

i should stay here now in kalymnos quite a while, i have brought my trunk here. all my things are in it. i may go for one month, in august, to crete; but then i would zoop right back to kalymnos.

there is another island right near by: astypallea; is famous for no snakes, no beetles, no this, no that. i would like as well to see this island. an old monk told the snakes to go away, and now if one even lands there, boom, he's finished. this island has as well no hotel, no restaurant, no cook-stove, no out-house, no pup-tent, no girl-scouts.

the house i live in has two eerie blue rooms with above the bed i sleep in a box full of ikons; all the island has to do, all the house has to do, all the *box* has to do is tremble and i am all over the head with ikons. i am only telling you this.

but i have the consolations of a solitary life. i stay in my cell and it becomes sweet. i have not yet stayed here long enough. imaginary phones is ringing all over the room. it is a quiet house. a nice, light blue little thing in the country. you must write me.

i close now, willingly.

yrs.,

Archbishop Mucculloch

XXIV THOMAS MERTON   *Oct. 31, 1964*

Ho

How long you think you can hide from the long arm of the postoffice? Where have you been? Have you grown the beard and put on the moppit and entered the sketes and lavras? Where is the long black vestment? Do you know that the sketes and lavras have missed the boat of aggirnamento or perhaps aggornamountain. Let the motto cry out from the captain's bridge as we sail round and round the Agios Horos: "Aggiorna-Mount-Athos." This pun will tickle the feet of the Protos.

Now I tell you I have a big exhibit of puns and calligraphies and soup spoons and artifacts and mobiles in Louisville I am in all the junk shops from November on with works of harp and artificials. I have made the picture, I have scooped the ink into a ball and flung it upon newsprnps and in pieces of picture. I have assailed the public conscience. It is the scandal of the evening according to all the prints of the borough. It should never have been allowed growls Juniper Johnson and the fiftieth plank of Coldbottle's platform is to decry the works of art by the Seven Stirring Mousewhip.

Now since truth is fancier than function I serve up from a manuscript from a lady in the Ky. mountains who writes about the danger she says the mental Mania. This that follows is copied from the original blue and red manuscraps of this lady who is very wild about the mental mania because the communists are coming to take all the good people and put them in a million acres of Alaska which have been specifically set apart for purposes of the mental mania. She says you can become a communist just by sitting at home in the bathroom.

Now here is the quotes, you better pay attention, because the Greeks have surely caught it too without you knowing a word of their subversions.

Here is literal truth quotes from Mrs. lady.

"Why hundreds of thousands of our people must be thrown into bondage just because Freud had to hit upon a money-making scheme to catch his girl; Think this over!

"Is evil overbalancing good today? In the USA?

"Next week I want to talk to you about how you can become a communist sitting right in your home.

"Quit going around repeating this Com. slogan half our poeple are insane.

"The person that is going to do something with an elderly person in their family because their eyes do not shine any more like a sixteen year old out on her first date.

"Why is Communism stronger in this state than any other state in the U.S.? Because Kentucky is a key state.

"It seems we are to be conformed into a bunch of mugged faced polly woggs." (Here is where I agree most.)

XXV. THOMAS MERTON   *Nov. 29, 1964*

Dear Rib or Bib:

Well Rob we are coming seriously to the end of another calendar year, and in fact we are already flung headlong into a new liturgical year as liturgy is quite fittingly ahead of the calendar since the spiritual is always ahead of the material. But Mob, at the end of a calendar year I want to talk to you about something I mean and you mean it too, I am sure, Mob, or Rob. In the name of our serious old college days then I want to ask you between you and me and conscience a serious question.

Now that you have been all this time in the isles of Greece I want to ask you, Rob, if you are still thinking American.

You know when we were in college we vowed we would always THINK BIG. We vowed it over the prostrate bodies of our drunken cronies besotted as they were with unamerican flippancies. HAVE YOU KEPT YOUR RESOLUTION? I HAVE. I am thinking Big rig or Mip, I mean Rob. I am Thinking Bibs in the rib. I think always of our 13 states and they make me think big. But you with those Greeks and orthos all around can you honestly say that you continue to think American? Have you not been infected with the smears of orthodox barbas and antique heathen liturgies to think SMALL, like small as some island like Kalympnis where you sem to be all the time? IS THAT BIG ENOUGH FOR OUR COLUMBIA DAYS? You know that the very name of our alma maigra signifies the gem of the notion and every boy that come out of that swamp thought Big and resolved to do his duty to think and BUY BIG. How can you BUY BIG in a little island where there is nothing for sale but shrimps and onions? You have given up your heritage for a mass of papas.

The other thing to ask yourself (always ASK BIG) is about "meaningful." Everybody around here goes about nodding and blinking about meaningful. Meaningful is a big psychiatric word that is the knot of the hub. Is the food you ate this morning meaningful? Is it meaningful NOW? Were you able to get Grapes Nut Flak in your grocer? NOT IN GREECE MAN. You can't tell me you got Grapes Nutsflak in GREECE. You have NOT THOUGHT BIG. Is your Grapenusflik meaningful? I bet if you ask yourself honestly well it ISN'T IT JUST ISNT.

Now i admit that although here in the monastery we think BIG we don't always think in grapenusflak and the life in every point is not always MEANINGFUL, though we try to put meaningful into the meaning of it. But there is something in the life nevertheless that makes you think BIG. And BUY BIG. And SELL BIG. But you know we are not selling as big this year as we did last? Someone in the office has begun to THINK LILL.

Well I just got to stop now. You remember that lady, that Kentucky lady, the one who wrote that book, remember? I told you some of her thoughts. JUST REMEMBER THOSE THOUGHTS. To someone like you I dont need to say no more than that. Just ask about meaningful and ASK BIG. Pass it on the Reinhardt to do the same. And try to tell the Greeks but you wont get noplace.

Cher Monty:

Dans le cours de 1965 il faut avant toutfoutre par terre les ithyphages et les tonitruants, sans parler de Baumstark et ses satellites. MAIS IL FAUT CONCENTRER LES FORCES DE LA NATION SUR LES MACHINATIONS INFAMES DE BAUMGARTEN.

(Quite the contrary we must deliver Baumgarten he is much maligned. He has been impressed into service by the ithypago!)

And now a party.

Ina lou I want you to meet Mary Fay meet Ina Lou Maryfay meet Irma, meet Irma Nan, hello Irma hello Ina Lou this is Irma Fay Mary Nan sit down hello the Lord be with you and with you too alleluia sit down again this is Henry.

Yes we have the new sing this is Margie Porter hello Margie sit down with the gang alleluia.

Hello Timmy are you coming over Mary Lou is here with her face come on over and bring Dodo.

This is Tiny Tim, Ina Moo, this is Lady Jane Grey, this is the fans, this is the electricity, this is the way up, this is the can, this is down, this is up, this is the whole house, sit down, have a coke, will you have a sevenup Marylou? What a wonderful party!

Yes we always have the latest and this is the latest. We have concentrated the latest on Baumgarten.

Mary Lou Baumgarten. Ina Fay, Anita Page, Myrna Loy Baumgarten, Ina Loy, Myrna Fay, Anita George, George Baumgarten. Allelulia. The latest is George. Meet hello. Metta fine baby doll hello alleluia.

What a marvelous party, I never had such a party in my life. We'll sing a poem and then the party will continue. I never had this party at all ever. It is a witch party, it is a false party, there never was any Ina Lou there never was any Mary Fay hello meet Ina Lou come on in sit down it is a wonderful party. Meet Margy Porter. Pass the canapes to Margy Porter. Quote Thomas Stearns Eliot and wash her feetses in soda water. Alleluia.

Bet you didn't have no such parties as this in Greece? Well we didn't have no such parties as this in Kentucky either. I was just musing on the general subject of parties.

Because we are in the season of parties and according to
Teilhard de Chardin parties is the Lord. Meet Teilhard de Chardin
he is mister excitement and he is now attending MIT. And with
you too, alleluia.

Earth satellites are falling like raindrops all over the mansions
of Tede Chardin. Hello this is Teddy, meet Chardin, he is mister
hullabaloo, he is attending Columbia U. Meet Ina Lou the prospect
of TC in Columbia flowers. What a devil of a party it was, it never
stopped until ten in the evening. Bet you had no such parties in
Greece this year or any other. Not since marathon was there ever
such a party, Happy new year, happy no jahr, who knows what
they have done with all the jahrgangs? It is Baumgarten, the old
rascal, he has stolen away the jahrgangs.

Well, let there be truth and beauty in Greeks for the prost
neujahr.

At least we can try to help Baumgarten, that is the least.
Alleluia.

Bestens.
Henry Clay.

XXVII. ROBERT LAX   *Kalymnos*

Hoy,

I am all right now—I am all over the party. Ina Lou is all over
the party. This is Lily Moustarsh. What do you think—we don't
have any parties? Mrs. Bindlestiff I want you should meet Mr.
Pflaum. Mr. Watchfob, Mrs. Novelty Stick-pin. Charms all over the
party. Up, down. This is the drawring room.

Our parties are noisier than yours, I'm sure. Charms, many an
axe-throwing fight at the parties. The lutanists come in from the
hills & throw their axes at the party.

This is Teilhard de Chardin—he's about to converge—everyone
at the party's about to converge. Better put your hat on because
everyone's going to converge. Mrs. Novelty Stick-pin is about to
converge with Mr. Rhinestone Clip.

Our parties are noisier (they're all full of Turkish delight) but I know what you mean. Everyone ought to think a lot more about parties

Yrs,

Chretien de Troyes

LIBEREZ LES BAUMGARTISTES

PART
TWO

Dear Most

Wabes have brought me yours numerous with syllabo i will think i will think.

Here is the facts.

I have wrotten you a proverb in plaint of fact with sybbalo. Sy-lla-bule.

Waves have brought me your numerous syllabus.

I will tell you what I think see proverbs.

There are some things too sacrd to mention but I have mentioned the facts in the spirit of industry.

What do I urge upon the youth manufacture i urge.

When you have read the proverbs you will see how it was urged but now i have to stop and send this on the waves.

I like what you say about the five o clock playa.

The waves in your place are safer.

Ask industry.

I will write more about manufacture in another day.

EVERYTHING I HAVE DONE HAS BEEN DONE FOR INDUSTRY.

What do I have to show for it?

Man-u-fac-ture.

You just ought to see my hands. They are covered with facts. That is why I type this with dermal gloves. My book of proverbs is the philosophy of manufacture by Dermal Glove.

That ought to be enough.

Next time in prose.

Meanwhile I think six houses is all right.

Here I manage with two: cenobite house,

hermit house.

More and more the latters.

Praise industry.

The world situation is the exceptional which proves the old rule: rigor mortis in the head has made Jack once more a soldier boy.

Try it out with a proof.

Lefty Gonxalo.

Book of Proverbs:
1. I will tell you what you can do ask me if you do not understand what I just said
2 One thing you can do be a manufacturer make appliances
3 Be a Man-u-fac-tu-rer
4 Be a manufac
5 Make appliances sell them for a high price
6 I will tell you about industry make appliances
7 Make appliances that *move*
8 Ask me if you do not understand what is move
9 First get the facts
10. Do not understand
11. Where to apply? Ask industry.
12. Do not expect to get by without Mr and Mrs Consumer
13 Man-u-fic-tion
14 I am wondering if you got the idea be a manu
15 Make other gods
16 Apply mind energy they will move
17 Mention one of the others see what happens
18 Now apply that to our problem
19 Try not to understand
20 Be a mounte-fictioner
21 Surpass all others in price and profit
22 Assail the public
23 Home-spun-facts-are-more-fun. Repeat it.
24 Prevent spreading on garments
25 Breathe more than others
26 Supply movement and traction
27 Our epidemix will exceed
28 A home made appliance: no honorable mention.
29 Now you can refer to garments and spread out
30 But there are more facts
31 For excitement: say whose epidemic may be next
32 Apply this to the facts and see what happens
33 Wear dermal gloves in bed
34 Here is an appliance that will terrorize mothers
35 And fight the impossible
36 Man-u-fac-ture: wear it on your head.

37 Wear dermal gloves on your head every morning
38 Beat it here come the mothers

II. ROBERT LAX

Bien cher Feuerbach,

i am prized with sorrow when i see that while i was off at the shootings in athens you were at that time fed by science in the hospital & forced to eat the ground-up innocuous foods. i am laffs again when i see that you are only a stumble across the hall from the co'colas & the milky ways, & that you are visited in your splatz by the tray-dropping jailbaits. this should not put you off in your thoughts. dropping a tray is only a way of asking for counsel. i know this because i had a great whale of a nurse once who dropped a tray, & i know she was asking for counsel.

the gut tangle, as you've rightly supposed, comes from thinking too much & living in the wrong country. i used to get it everytime i'd set foot on the island of new york. this would often end up in the hospital, the clickity-click down the hall & the wavery appearance of your friends in the recovery room.

it is good if they only feed you the mashes. you must be obedient to the mashes & the milky ways. always swallowing down the one & not neglecting the other. & you must act benignly, like a benign 50-year old author, toward the small trembling girls & you will not be sorry. very small girls, like 8 & 10, stand outside the door & call my name all day. they do not invite me to their parties yet, but i know they will.

i too am full of hostility, even on kalymnos, but most of the time it does not make knots in my stomach. a good thing, too, because the only hospital they have around here is for fish. if a fish looks bad, they take it off to the hospital & make it look good. but there is no such thing as a greek looking bad. if a greek looks bad, he's dead.

what i mean is that there is no such thing as a greek either looking or being tired. getting tired is something that seems to happen to strangers. sometimes they get tired of greeks. greeks never get tired of anything.

one other thing about greeks: anything any greek can do, *any*

---

greek can do. whether it's making yaourti, mending nets or catching fish with your bare hands, if one greek can do it, any greek can. this makes it different from a country in which one man is a dentist & another can breathe.

now to our things: i am glad you found that big fat book & sent it. none of the things have arrived yet, but it is that very big fat book you just found that i think i wanted. (i'll be able to see soon enough if i wanted it, now.) emil has found two other books he wants to print, and i think they may be better. i like to write these books & have him reach into the cellar every once in a while & print one up. i more & more think that writing is like talking to yourself & that all you can hope to do is improve the level. (these days i talk to myself in foolish imperatives, & all it does is run me into trouble.)

as i say to myself: 'you must go to the movies.' this is all right, but then it turns out there aren't any movies on tuesday. you're lucky there are plenty of milky ways in the hall. as well as the old souvenir girl who cheers up the fathers. you realize of course that the playwright lope de vega based his whole career on less of an insight than that. i will come & visit her personally. we will sell it to the burlesques.

let me know if you are in or out of the hosp. let me know about the disc slip, too. is that all right? is it better? is it slipped back in place? 50 years is not very old for an author. you must stand on your head as much as possible & take care of yourself.

yrs,
Cardinal Mundelein

III. THOMAS MERTON   *Oct. 16, 1965*

Dear Russ and Bill.

Well you are probably wondering why I haven't written from the camp for so long. I'll tell you about it. The camp has been on fire for months. It all started in the flypaper factory where I was chief in charge of Trappist fly paper a communist front organization numbering millions. I'll tell you about the millions some other time. The fire began in the *imperatives* section.

Let me tell you about our imperatives section. Just a moment.

Let me tell you about it. The best way to tell you is to tell you our product. We make imperatives. They are like fly paper. A simple imperative is "Stay on the flypaper Jack or just try to get off anyway" that is one of our more simple imperatives. I made millions. Each imperative is a communist front. Behind the flypaper is a communist fly who is not on paper. He is classified. That suggests another imperative: *Classify that insect!* Some day I will send you a page of our products. We have a million imperatives. We invented THINK and we invented the funny communist front version THIMK which every laughing business hat has on his desk. Here comes another imperative: CLASSIFY BUSTER. They come out like that.

Now to tell you the truth Sam I am living as a stylite on top of a hermit hat which I got in the woods as a result of having been myself classified out of existence in the flypaper department. I am living as a hermit. I am utterly alone from all human company except the Nigra on the Cream of Wheat Box and he is the only Nigra in the USA who still knows his place. That is why I am here with no other company than this Nigra who knows his place which is on the Cream of Wheat box and no place else. The place of Nigras is on boxes of this type and no other for example the Aunt Jemima pancake box. WHO LEFT ALL THEM NIGRAS OFF THE BOXES? That comes from the question department but it can easily become an imperative if you make it imperative. I leave it to you, right now I am only suggesting. One of my most successful imperatives was *Promote boot fetishism.* I think of it often while I am promoting boot fetishism. Also glove fetishism. I wrote in another poem about the dermal gloves. I have millions of dermal gloves, some left gloves some right gloves, usually more of one than the other. One of my imperatives is STOP THAT GLOVE which I have to use when the gloves escape. Another imperative I have which is more a suggestion put in the form of a question, but is timely none the less: ARE WE GOING TO LET CAL COOLIDGE GET AWAY WITH IT? Put that in your pipe and smoke it.

Did you get all the cookies and goodies I sent in the form of disguised hats and manuscripts? Did you get the tame muskrats? Did you get the fee? Did you collect the tenth part of the ephod? I mean the ephi? I got to go and put on the ephod right now. That must be why I had it in mind. Before I go I got another imperative WRITE DAD NOW. Who knows, maybe there is a letter in the

Cream of Wheat box. But this is just to let you know I make no more cookies in the cookie factory, I am out here with the lizards. Nobody is mad and it is all okay. I am sorry about Margie Rice but there is nothing I can do about it. I am sorry about Ed he should come down but he didn't he went to a rival outfit. Now I close with our product: PUT DOWN THAT SWORD AND LISTEN TO ME. This was copyrighted by an earlier play of the poet Dante in which he says "For the woman ze kees, for the man ze sword." Here are some other new imperatives HAVE FRET TODAY — EAT MORE CAT — BUILD FOR FIDO — DISCARD BLUES WITH TOOTSIE HOME FUN — WAKE LON WITH NEWS — EAT THAT STATEMENT AND SMILE — OBEY MEN OF GOD — SHOW WHY NUNS VANISH — REVEAL OPPORTUNITY TO LAME BRAIN UNCLE — NEEDLE THE FUTURE LEADER — I got a million more where those came from but I got to go put on the ephod and listen for news. BETTER DUCK WHEN THE NEWS ARRIVES. Seriously it is nice to be out here in the beach with nothing around but the breezes and aunt.

    CONCENTRATE

    Relax. Breathe out.

IV. THOMAS MERTON   *Nov 10, 1965*

Ho:

    What you mean Fitzsimmons [F] is an indiangiver and an accepter but not a printer: have you seen the Lugano Rev? It just fall into my hous the Lugano Rev and what do I find? Nothing but you for mile after mile, never say Fitz was an indiangiver. [*James Fitzsimmons had just published Lax's* Sea and Sky, *a long poem, in a double issue of the* Lugano Review.] He was a smart cat knew he had a good thing when he had one and he gave it the best. You deserve the best and the best is what you got. Them poem is most exciting they blow off the top of the hat sitting on that white sheet. One could do many drawings on the whitesheet but for reverence let nobody do any drawing let them just stop and think you made use of all that silence it falls into the silence just one word on top of another fast not with undue hesitations it move right along about the city, and the people with the vain they was muttering. It

---

moves right along with the sea being a yearning sea I think this is the best poem we got flying around and Fitz done give it his best, and I don't mean his best Indian.

By now you have in your hand the Lugano and you have eat your mouth for saying he gave you the Indian.

But never mind I understand I have said the same myself many a time and after that I eat my mouth on account of the false Indian.

Your two poems is most impress.

You are right about the city and about the sea. Your message has struck home.

Now you should find a man with all that paper to make a book and from the note I judge Emil is that man.

You say he gave you an Indian: well that Indian had a fortune in oil wells. That was the kind of Indian he was giving. Praise Fitz for the Indian friend he gave you.

You looked the gift Indian in the mouth and found he was drunk with good fortune.

You found him flying in a golden acroplane.

You said he would not come but he came in a chariot of cloud and fire dispensing oilwells to friends.

You said you was forsook and what did you get? Texas to print on. That's all.

Never mind, that's the way it is with us Indian writers. It comes from writing everything and seeing everything in Chippewa.

I am moved to emotions and I am fallen on the floor with sighs and transports because I have receive from the women who fasted in Rome for peace a paper they all writ while fasting, they signed it all with fasting fingers saying be our friend. How should I not be friend of these fasting ladies who have moved the whole Council up ten notches closer to God and make them speak of peace and kept silence the American Bishops from jumping up and yelling about bombs and war. They have shut up that fool Bishop Hannon with their fasting and they deserve praise, let them think of me any time they want I am ready to be thought of kindly by such ladies. Tomorrow Mass for the peace, but the mists of bad feeling are all over this country let me tell you it smell bad here in Denmark. Peace with the Indian.

Ho Mopsuestio:

This is the afternoon for resolutions. Nice sunny bright holiday afternoon but I chopped wood to keep the house convenable with a medium chauffage. Here is it middle chauffage with woods heat and superchauffage with cutting up the woods it all adds up to plenty chauffage except in the middle of the night when the woods all sleep and the jackfrost climbs in the window with a wink and a blink. I think I sent you a message jackfrost is thought to pass up Kalymnos. Well did he? Here anyways is the chauffage. So much for practical inserts. Now for business ventures.

First resolution of bright afternoon: you didn't get the letters, your letters, my letters, all typed up by lady in California who wants to join the nuns but happens is not catholic which is considered by nuns troublesome. No envy to be Catholics just nuns. Anyways, back to the letters. She typed them all up, right? And I sent them, right? To Venice or some dam place I sent them, to Pizza, to them pensiones you was at, to Father McGough [*Father Thomas McGlynn, Dominican sculptor then living in Pietrasanta, near Pisa.*] in Italy, I sent the letters, right? Well, you never got them. Now I got another copy, plus one for me. Now what I do is I put the copy with this letter. Now read carefully: if you are reading this letter you got *all* the letters. Because they are all under this one and the whole tribe of letters is register, is insured, is c.o.d., is air freight, is come by refrigeration (I got chauffage on the mind). YOU HAVE ALL THE LETTERS. I thought I would send you all the letters. Thus if you finally got the others from Venice, which I doubt, as nothing ever comes further than Venice when it once stops there, then if you got the others and these both you got two copies, but two is better than one. All I want though is for you to have one. Now you got it, I hope, unless this is rocked in the cradels of the deep or something worse eaten by the polaris submarine. Do not let the letters out of your sight they are worth a fortune.

Second resolution: I had this picture lying around here for two months waiting to send. It is proof of the superior wisdom of the horse. Maybe Gladio [*Gladys Marcus, Lax's sister in Olean*] and Mary Davis send you this same horse months ago. I have no care for their foresights, I send you the same horse also, for its wisdom, twice is better than once, but I want you to see this wise horse at least once. I don't have no mexican newsprints so I send you the horse. A superior being is this horse. Let all praise the horse. So much for the second resolution. Do not let this horse out of your sight he is too dam wise to be left out of sight. This horse has to be watched.

I have watched this horse for two months and he has got wiser all the time, he is now so wise I am sick of it, fed up I tell you. I take no more back talk from this horse even though it be a college graduate. It is a faithless beast, but the lady deserves no less than she get. He gave her what she had coming to her. That is still only part of the second resolution.

After these two I am all out of important resolutions. I may have a three, let me see something about Jules Verne. Read Jules Verne, but not you. How can anybody get Jules Verne in Kalymnos. Skip it. That wasn't the one.

For the mice, no resolution. You got a smart landlady, she is a cat, she can take care of everything. Not everbody got a cat for a landlady. She will take care of the mice never fear. Don't give it another thought. I got no cat. The mice are on the porch. They are in the woodpiles, and I would perhaps put them in the chauffage but they are smart, they are all college graduates. But they do not talk back. No further resolutions required as to mice.

Anymore resolutions? We American citizens have had enough of President Johnson and of Secretary McNamara as also of J. Edgar Hoover. That for the govt.

Back a few weeks ago I was send you a joke I thought up about Moe on the Mt which run through my mind whiles I was chopping wood for the chauffage. But it was unseemly to make jokes about Moe on the Mt (a religious subject) during the Advents. Now it is come the holiday season and one can loosen up a bit about the jokes even on religious subjects (or objects) such as Moe on the Mt, but I have forgotten my quips. No matter, not much of a quip anyways. Leave Moe on the Mt. No trouble. Forget all about this resolution it is otiose.

I was send Fitz simmon a long tiresome joke about Zens. I don't know if I send you. It is called the Zens Koan. It supersedes all that has been said to the same effect in the last month by me or by my landlady. It is the Zen Koan. You get busy and let me know if you didn't get it. It will scare the mice nearly to death if you

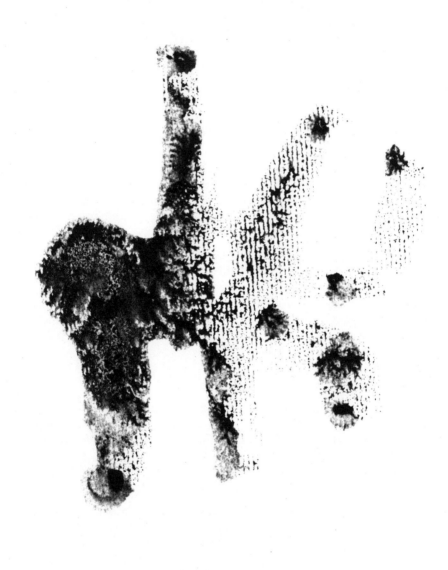

leave it lying around. Just leave it lying around.

So much for the mystics. That is about all I got this Tues. If it comes back about Moe I will remind myself not to tell you because it was a poor piece of wit and not seemly.

I read always of hermits. Bl Godric work day and night on his chauffage and his axe was heard ten miles in dead of night. I think it is a trumped up tale of Bl Godric. His sister had a hermitage down the road a little and when she hear the bell at his place(or the axe maybe she was driven crazy by that axe) she flopped down and prayed but didn't dare to go near his mass. I guess he would have chased her out with the whip or something. She came close but no closer than was safe she knew what was good for her. It was a trumped up tale about the axe ten miles at night. Another hermit was old and infirm and he worked in his garden with a cane. I tell myself I don't need a garden and when it comes to the cane I will have to have the angels provide the chauffage, but trust, trust. Maybe it was another trumped up tale about that cane. What do you think?

Tristan and Isolde went to the hermit as fast as their legs could carry them when they were in a fix on account of that medicine. Wise thing to do. Hermit said you shd never have taken that medicine and other good advice, no trumped up hermit he. Good counsel was his motto and he gave it. But what was the result? I forget.

I don't know what more except there is a lady in Canada who is pulling strings to get Bramachari [*Hindu monk and friend of Merton and Lax*] into the country only Bramachari went around the block in his place and found himself a prisoner in Pakistan, so there he sits in Pakistan. Should never have crossed the street. Nevertheless the lady keeps pulling strings. She writes me a funny letter about where she was in a Zen place and got satori and all the roshis couldn't believe it and they were talking about her in Japanese and here she was all the time Catholic. All she could hear them saying was satori and katoliks. She had them guessing.

Now it is time for the frugal supper and secret holiday goodies tucked in the back of the icebox. Another lady made rich goodies stuffed into an orange which nearly causes death I will now stand around in front of the icebox for ten minutes wondering whether to eat another one. Gone is the old decision. I stand nonplussed in front of the secret goodies which may be deadly. Faugh. I can find better goodies than that. No trouble. Do not worry, I have the chauffage and the supper, up to a point. The rest is only figments.

The secret of the hermit life is that it remove the foundations and take away the building and there is no roof left and one float down the stream like a chip in the waters. I think you find this in Kalymnos, it not no matter. All is tasteless say John of the Crux. If not, no matter.

Felix neujahr.

VI. ROBERT LAX   *kallinbrooks january 5 66*

Dear Fred or Wolfgang.

i was in happiest receipt of yours that had the horse, & all the letters & all your news & that came registered in spite of all the greek authorities & italian authorities & how many other fellows with caps over there with the blacks & whites. what the horse say to the lady we must say every one to his rider; & most especially to that great white rider in the black house who's now tramping rough shoes over the hopes of the world: you heard us: beat it.

i am glad, as i say that it came registered & didn't end up in some mailman's gondola. you live on an island like this long enough & you start to think that nothing, nothing, nothing will ever arrive, that even the ads are intercepted, that nobody ever will send anything unless maybe someday a sandwich drifts by in a bottle. but here they are, every one of our letters. i could sit & read them forever.

& here is page 3. i thought page one & page 3 had gone by the skiff, but here is page 3. what is the late from e cardenal & from alvaradez guinsberg. i write to cardenal 3 years ago in colombia, but the runner has never come back. perhaps he is in nicaragua where the fun is. or else in colombia where the fun is.

i hope i can find again the story of mr dimitriades who lost 17 million dollars worth of jewels by throwing them into a dustbin in Athens & recovered them (at a cost of 17 million dollars) by recourse to a crane, a police cordon, the department of sanitation & his own (& his relatives') natural tears. i will find it; i will send it; you will see.

send me too (now that advent is over & before lent begins)

your thoughts of mt. morris. i walk around the hermitings all day wondering how a thought of mt morris would first begin.

i hear the voice of bl. godric, appsey-bo pappsey-bo; i hear the voice of blessed godric axing down the night.

must close now. stay away from the stuffed pimentos. i'll give them your best at the roundhouse.

Sam

GET (THAT IS DON'T FAIL TO GET)

LET-TERS OF WM SHAKE-SPEAR TO SIH MOM

MR SHAKE-SPEAR'S CON-TRI-BU-TION TO ELIZ-A-BETH-AN CUL-TURE

IS OF COURSE IN-ES-TI-MA-BLE . . . CAR-DIFF DAIL-Y HER-ALD

VIa. ROBERT LAX

well, here it is days later in a brand new house: the home of aspasia & pericles. old house has been torn down & put up again, torn down & again put up. no neighbors here, no one to care. sponge-clippers clip downstairs: clip-clip, exchanging their views.

aunt writes from australia. she lives in the woods. few berries, she says, at this season, but no matter: she has no (can't make it out). seems to be all right (bicycles into the village) & sends you her best.

No I never got the Koans. the minute you get a second away from the mice, you send me a koan. i moved away from my mice. they were beating on the plates with spoons. more forage. more cakes & plaster. it is better for us all i moved away. send the koans right away; i am starting a spring semester.

(the other day i open up a box of sardines & all of a sudden it comes to me clear: the old days...lita mc kinley, victor mc glaglen..the barberry room; i stand there holding the box & could hardly have cried.)

i hear the ax of Bl Godric, hoopsaboy, hallelujah; i hear the ax of Blessed Godric, zowie, zowie, bam. (i hear the voice of Godric's sister: zowie, zowie, bam, hallelujah. i hear the voice of Godric's sister: zowie, bam, bam, bam.)

VII. THOMAS MERTON   Jan. 28. 1966

Dear Rops:
I have in hand your aimable aeroporikos written on aspasia with fred. Yes it is wise to register I am glad all the letters is now safe behind the authorities and not being scrutinized in the polizei of venice ever the worst was the polizei of venice. Your thoughts for the great white rider in the what's house if true is right for the horse, every horse. No more stomping on the hopes of the world. Beat it from the what's horse, and further abscond from the blacks and whites, your puzzles are of no use. As for the mailman's gondola, damn it I say.

Every one of the letters is now safe, I can relax. Typed by poor lady in the cellars of santa barbara or someplace, wore out her eyes, now is the tutti frutti of worn out eyes: the happy author sits and wonders. Tutti frutti is all she will ever more get from that achievement.

I open so many boxes of sardines every minute I hardly have time to think of the old days. Maybe if it was cocacola with the sardines I would think of the old days with McGargle and McGonigle on the hill top. How did we ever keep warm on the hill top? Here I rush madly all day with the axe and exhaust my flagging spirits with bringing in yule logs. Then when I open the sardines finally late at night I am so exhausted I have no further memories of the old days of McGargle Conklin McKinley that old plaster.

How come you got all them aunts in australia when I got all them aunts in newzealand all knitting sweaters like frantic to keep me from the berries? I mean the berry berries. So it always was with aunts anyway.

Now here is honest news: Ed Rouse [*Rice*] was here, sent by the table of contents, and came with the camwraps and the appareil. We opened up the sardines dutifully but it did not come back any of the old days, we are all too serious now for the old days, there is so much of the new days, so vast, so heaped up, so oppressive, so lamentable, that there remains no time for the old. Rush rush rush say the new days, rush over the falls with us. And who can say them nay? Not all our old friends. Gerdy as you know he gone. [*Robert Gerdy, friend and classmate, later an editor of* The New Yorker, *died of a heart attack.*] Poor Gerdy he done gone. They got Gerdy when he walked out of his apartments, I mean them, they, the fates, Clotho McSweep. And all them.

Others is all went. Arthur Farrish has gone. Photofinish Pound is wound up for the last, a winner in the end. Mother McCrea—gone. Sappho Sweeny is however still all over the theaters, you can't stop Sappho Sweeny. Just try. She not gone. All the rest but not her.

I kick the mice out of the way and send Koans so fast they upset all the gondolas between here and Grips.

Now it is winter and the snow lies deep and what is on the front porch beside the mice? All the feathered tribe is on the front porch, too numerous too stupid and too agitated for civil words. With the feathered tribe I have innumerable differences of opinion. First I serve the feathered tribe soda crackers, which they gobble up with a hopscotch and a bump. Silly little rumps up and down all over the porch, jump sideways to push each others off from a crumb, silly birds I cry in desperation but I have to laugh At which having run out of sodacrackers what do I do? Put out Mother's Orange Rings. What you think happened next? they taste the first crumb of mothersorangerings and whap, they fly away in terror in every direction north south east and west into the blue zero. Never saw such a reaction before. I rush out and cry come back it is only mother but to no avail. Never catch me eating another mothers orange ring as long as I live, them birds must *know*.

So watch the bottles as they drift by and if they have in them mother's orange ring no matter how loud and how vain they shout twenty nine cents do not touch it. Now further about Bro Godric it has come to me that I doubt Bro Godric but do not doubt his sister. What should I do? (It must be the sister with the ten mile axe zowie zowie whap.)

Now the latest from Cardenals is that he is ordained and is in Nicarea making a hostel on a small Nicaroan island where there is contemplations, flutes, coffee beans, small boa constrictors and man eating sharks but otherwise all is at peace. Write him box 206 Managua Nicaragua. He will tell you about the feathered tribe as it is in Niconcagua also the finny tribe which is dreadful there.

You find the story of Mtr Dimitriades and the jewels I need bad just that story. Meanwhiles I send you the arts of vote, how the boy was uneasy singing the serenade (well might they be uneasy these boys with their serenades) how the poverello was surprised by the ox, how the military was made safe, all the votes and more they are the supreme art there is none better you will never in your life after this want to see any other.

Do not give a thought to Mt Morris first second third or last. The last in this case should come before the first. Mt Morris I am convinced is all akimbo but not so much akimbo as this typewriter it is fiendish this typev.riter it scrambles ribbons into knots pieces of it get up and run away in the middle of a word it is a machine I detest this appareil. Back to Mt Morris I would say never even give a thought to that akimbo community, where they all come out and stand with their arms akimbo looking for Tom Swift to ride through on his electric weasel. What a way to spend the time. It is a fools paradise, that is my first and last thought about Mt Morris. It is a quandary also, so that everyone who lives in Mt Morris is of necessity in a quandary. There is no such place as Mt Morris it is a will of the whisp. Imagine the folly of the people who have been enticed into this non-existent trailer camp under the pretext that it is a place to live. The gangsters in the end will run away with their trailers and they will be none the wiser for all their mount and all their Morris. They should thereafter live only in a place with one name, not two. Mount this, valley that, pah, they are all frauds these mountains and these valleys, filled to the top with gangsters all of them. You are better off in Greece think no more of Mount Morrish.

72

I have to stop before I hit this typewriter with an axe you will hear from here to Greece. Long live the sister of Bl Godric. Farewell.

VIII. ROBERT LAX   *patmos*
                                                    hir is patmos

cher murps,
    hir again is holy patmos. patmos really holy place. what i mean dear murthwog, it's what i'd call a holy place. holy, that is, not at all like the elks. & place; like the place is holy. not saying something one way or another about the people. maybe they are too. maybe they all are. but the place. flowers, rocks birds. it's more like the rocks look happy.
    birds too, very good. only place i ever see birds. sweep, swoop. nobody pinging at them must be part of it. (but why not? isn't there any greeks on this island?)
    here the crocodile rooster lays his egg.
    here the bird-dog tinkles after the woolly sheep.
    i will stay in patmos week after week. pages will fly from the calendar pops. i will still be here.
    yrs,
    Sam

IX. THOMAS MERTON   *Feb 15, 1966*

Dear Robs:
    You have invited me to the Deans Day Delirium (DDD) for 1966 and you have said Make Big the DDD. Could it be bigger? Even the prospect of it is already a monster. Make bigger with Harry J Friedman [*another classmate; was business manager of the* Columbia *Jester*] Make bigger with Randall [F] on the moon, and if there are men beyond solar system says another? How big is all the sapnaku pardon the san paku that will be prevalent in all the participants at the end of DDD? They will stagger even before it has all begun and where will they be at the end? The whites of their eyes are already showing in every direction, they have whites

of the eyes on the tops of the heads, they have whites of the eyes all the way down to the chin so much has become already the sanpaku [*Japanese: vitamin deficiency, fatigue and "excessive showing of the whites of the eyes"; all-cereal diet is recommended as cure.*] contrary to the book of Daniel. Let them read the book of Daniel and find what was the diet of the lions and nobody noticed whether or not the lions had sanpaku. This holy Japanese doctor he is right: all the young doctors american trained die in Japan and all the old Zen men sit around to a ripe old age because they sit in the zendo and think of the corban. Still I cannot but be carried away and with you I exclaim make Deans Day Big, this by making small every other concern. We must approach this with strict logic as Mr Randall would have it and Mr Nagel and Dr Guttman and El Brendel who was never on the faculty in my time. Well would you not know that Harry J Friedman was behind it all? And you ask that we make it big? Let it be made big already by Giant Friedman.

Now to other topics. I like your bust of Old Black Joe. It is marvelous for coherence. How did you ever do it? Such subtle insights. You have covered up all the racial charactristics but yet it is unmistakably O.B.J. But he is not to be in Bardstown for the dean on this or any other day. The dean never has a day in Bardstown. Bardstown is both too small and too unhealthy for a deans day and the people are all too drunk with eyes closed to have sanpaku. How does one diagnose sanpaku when the eyelid is always closed? Yet I will get that book, but let me tell you if you are going to see Rice be careful what he sees you eating, he turned me in to the detectives for eating sardines, good old sardines like the old days, no memories turned me in to the detectives. Forward with the Dean.

IXa. THOMAS MERTON

Today I said to Mrs Who
Lady you got the sanpaku
Throw that coffee pot away
Do like I say
And go to bed
Go to bed
With postum Throbbing through the head
No beer and wines upon the bib
No sankas on the under lip
Take that bottle off yr hip
Lady you got the sanpaku
Let me tell you what to do:
You go to bed
Go to bed
With postum throbbing through your head.

Today I said to Mrs Why
Madam you are about to die
You must go to Doctor Jap
To learn why coffee giveth clap
Your crazy hair is going blue

Your eyes though glass are sanpaku
So go to bed
Go to bed
With sea weed wrapped around your head.

Today I said to Mrs Clay
Meet you Momma on Dean's Day
With Harry Friedman sanpaku
Randall and Uncle Guttman too
Run run run run run run run
To see the fun.
To see the fun.

Make it big
With Harry and the old nun.

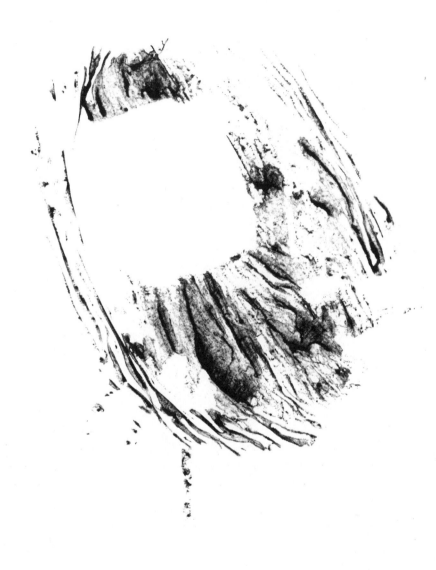

Dear Commodore Perry,

The minute the bird flew in with your scripts i was thrown on the floor with hilarity; such was my joy that i beat my fists on the floor until the spongeclippers (silent, surly men who work downstairs) said i should either cut it out or move. yes, there is always somebody downstairs; did aristotle have somebody down stairs too? did pericles? here is always someone except at night. at night, if i wasn't so tired, i could dance & sing.

the other night i am dancing & singing with gypsies. the gypsies are dancing & singing too, sizing up my pockets & asking me how much i make. i give them satisfactory answers & all in the romany tongue. i think i will now be friends of a sort with the gypsies.

i take some pictures of these gypsies. they look exactly like mr dimitriades. & here, indeed, then, is mr. dimitriades. he has fired his niece. she will never be left to sit on the treasures again. (it is important to read the parables and to understand their conclusions.) this is the parable for mr dimitriades.

everyone of your treasures is newly arrived: the typescripts of santa barbara's sister: i have not yet read them; the koans, i have only begun; but the votive pictures i am reading every day. every day, new treasures: the tuscan oafs & their serenade; the married couple whose cart has turned over: the married couple, you will note, is saved; the horse is upside down forever. (this is how it sometimes seems to us all.) here is a man who has fallen down stairs & has scarcely had time to raise his arms in prayer. (he, too, is saved.) & here is a poor man attacked by an ox; his wife & her brother can not drive him out with their pitchforks; but one of these jets a cry of great force to the heavens & now (panel 2) the bestia fugge via.

a veritable treasure house: i will not let my niece come near it. here is a devout man fallen from a hoist; here is a young one fallen in the river; here is rider who has been thrown from his horse; & here is luigi again with the ox.

but now let us hurry back to dean's day where old black joe is waiting in the whathouse. here is moses hadas in the rushes (that is the mt. morris joke i was asking about: not mt st morris, but let it go, let it go) what you say about mt st morris is true. & here is uncle gutberg who will carry the first translations of schiller & feuerbach to the moon.

last year's deans day was pretty exciting too: i didn't get there but i read about it. the mark van doren prize (this true) was awarded to dwight w. miner as being the one left on the faculty who was most like mark van doren. (developments followed in dizzying succession:) the irwin edman prize was (tossed like a hot penny) to john hermann randall; the moses hadas prize was given to james i gutmann; the barzun-trilling prize shot back & forth between barzun & trilling, but was finally walked off with by harry j carman. as a last thing (just before the march began) the dwight w. miner prize was given to dwight w. miner, as being the most like everyone else on the faculty.

nothing in it for old black joe. mama's orange rings for old black joe. mama's rumpskin bird rings for old black sam & i'sa cummin. that's how it's always been.

this brings us now with startling rapidity to the koans: i have only read a few the koans, but have already started a free interlinear translation of some for our next minstrel blowout at the elks (& ladies of the elks) club jamshanks:

O B Joe: you drink "dat" ribber i'll answer "yo" question.

O B Sam: i dun drink "de" ribber.

O B Joe: i dun answer "yo" question.

it'll take a little work & plenty of practice, but we got some natural actors at the elks.

aunt, i must have told you, is still working in the bindery. somebody's written a book about nakomis. not much other news around the bathysphere.

i'll write again soon & send more dispatches. here's one already about 3 old ladies & a loup; not much of a story, but a nice cast of props. hey: i am seeing you in all the papers. will write you soon about all the papers.

Sam

Dear Senator:

Before I run to the hosps it has come your missips with the
gypsies with old black joe and with the treasure of dimitriades
playin on the roof. Old Black Joe lucky to be the garbage man
found the treasure playing in the gargle and in a tinkle I mean
twinkle solved every koan like this:

O.B.Joe: Who was that lady I seen you with last night?
O.B.Sam: Dat was old man Ribber, he name Dimitriades.

Curtain falls indiscriminately on Joe and Sam there is all mixed up
the races and another koan is solved. NEXT.

Master: Who was that treasure I seen you with last night?
Disciple: Garbage you old bum.

Curtain falls indiscriminately on Master and disciple and everybody
gets fifty whacks of the ossu. I mean the bossu. Everybody dance
the bossu, curtain falls through the floor. What a mess is these
Zens. Nothing is orderly any more.

Dancing the bossu
On top of the hossu
Old Man Ribber
And cosa nostra
Solve the conundrum
Three's too many
To dance the bossu
On top of the hossu.

Everybody gets fifty whacks of the conundrum. Nothing solved.
Begin again.

Now here is the news of the day about the book of the year. The
book of the year is the reading of the evening while I solve hossus
and eat my frugal suppers sitting at the window and munching on
all the rivers I have swallowed in one day. What is the book of the
year? YOUR book is of the year the very book. It is the great book
of each evening it was come from Mark Doorstops with encomiums
too far short of the truth. It is the Everest of Journals. It is the
Kachenjunga of Poems. It makes me want to throw over everything
especially the back operatio and come to Kalumpups. You got
plenty social life in Kalopsis. Now it is gypsies the social life, now
dinner in the ships, now ouzos in the cafe now the spinning lady
for which I have deepest respect the spinning lady has beaten all

the hossus and just sits quiet and spins with the Buddha mind.
Doesnt know this.
Here's what I do. I hide your treasure in garbage and I put in the
hands of New Direction. How about that? How about I give them
your book. I gonna send yo old man book to Joe at New
Perfections. It will be an eyeopener for the dustraps in the parlor of
New Distinctions. Let me send yo old junnel into the New Tunnel
of Perfections.
Yassuh Junnel
Right down the Funnel
Laughing and singin
All de day long
Up and down de Sewanee Review
til Gabriel blow
dat HAWN.
Serious I send the junnel into the New Perceptions and it will
cause to explose all the mimic business of the whole New Walk. I
cause the junnel to form in the eyeslips of the sankapus up and
down the New Yak pulse.
I cause the Junnel to quicken the traffic in every tunnel with crazy
mad runs to the frontshops and buy more junnel.
I make rich the Kapympops no need anybody to hide the treasure.
What I like in the junnel is where de old man in the ribber say he
got to turn aside and get one last sponge.
Dat is de parable of the funnel all right.
O.Joe: Who was dat ol black ribber I seen you wit las mitternacht?
O.Sam: Dat no mitternacht you dam fool that de RIBBER.
Curtains of journals fall indiscriminately on New Directions,
Harpers. Doubletake, Skimpers, Sahibs, Shade and Wart, Covici
Friede, Anna Christie, etc etc.
Who dat old black marbles I seen you with playing on the roof?
Dat no roof, dat the top of de mawnin white boss (St Patricks Day
Jk) Joke of cat and mama playing on the roof I laff and laff I
swallow another river while laffing. I will tell it to all the monks as
a parting shot as I creep under the anesthetics.
You will find deans day exactly in the same shapehouse as it was
before.
"DE" shapehouse, what other?
"DE" fine old man ribber.
Old Man ribber just keep rowing the lawn.

Yo ho ho and a barrel of Joe
He just keep rowin "yo" Laaaawwwwnnn.
You think it is a joke of the old ladies but it was no joke for
reynard the props. No sour grape he! Crushed with canes. He
wished he never begun. But the point is this: back of my hermitage
is fifty apartment houses twenty stories high all foxes. In the
summer the foxes go rabid and bite the hermits on sight, rush up
gang on the house singing old man ribber and bite the hermit with
rabies this is a sly joke for when I come back with no back. I got
the sanpaku book and since then I have give up not coffee no not
coffee only just the sugar thassall. I make the coffe like the Greek
skippu or whatever it was you say. I throw the sanpaku book at
the heads of all diets. I am through with food. Look carefully at all
the ex voto pictures and you find out how to beat sanpaku, and
still drink coffee.
Bury deans day with Carman and Edman say I.
After I wrote the crazy inept joke about Mount St Morris it came to
me an agle I mean angel and he said severe "It was not Mt Kisco
the man said you idiot." Such is bird life in this zone.

    Harpo.

XIa. THOMAS MERTON

Instructions exhortations and imperatives
Find out regulator in gear seven.
Up town six pay belle.
Invent more feelings for Pop Latin.
Here you are brother set this all on the foe table.
Cramp heads and run for liturgy.
Stop that indicator and set dry flange then crump & count then
until you meet (WOW) azimuth. Watt theology guaranteed slit
second illusions of lifted hope. Mum it, mum it twice and humble
preserve theology slant from backwaps first rate self forget. This is
Mystic guide to shanty hep. Again I say it: Azimuth (WOW).
Follow with a crash and transport subject into home. NEXT.
Here you are bathers and pets wanted.
How to beat balmy: with trust funds.
A man who accumulates and looks ahead can scarcely discern the

front flap of the pocket feed.
Cheese it the gypsies.
There is something about circumstance that is all american.
Flip the ammo to mother nature and consort.
Meet Mister Prose Howdy Joe.
Emphasize Mommas new orange order and ring for bird.
Time to go and pay toll to Lefty.

XII. ROBERT LAX

june 1 66
hooray for thornton w. burgess

Dear Captain Bashford,

this is likely to be a short, fitful note: the only kind the birds
have been uttering, too. it is the weathers. they have really
monkeyd too much with the skies, and now in greece when it
should be sun is all rain, howling winds & other manifestations
formerly kept for the germans. gloom, for example, once an
exclusive property of the north woods, has lately been sliding over
the jugoslav border. (the jugs have been distilling it for years with
prune-pits into a national drink called weltschmerz, which really
isn't so bad for the first few hours.) but here in joyous greece, the
happy isles, nobody knows what to make of it. (no one but me.)

reinhardt has been to the virgin islands. reinhardt has seen
gibney [F; *Gibney was then living in St. John*] & gibney reinhardt.
they have seen each other up & down. & each hath seen with
amazement the children of the other. i have no other news, except
that givney has an old, very old, rattle-trap car, & the car bit
reinhardt.

from slate [F], no news, no news at all. when last i seen him
he was just coming up from under a heart's attack; but i think he is
all well now.

& you're the one who keeps in touch with seymour.

(have the pakistanis ever released bramachari? i wish he would
walk past here on his way to boston.)

(it was nice, what they said about gerdy in the new yorker.)

there isn't too much of the old crowd left around the k of c.

now let's see; i moved from down by the fishes to up in the
hills. it's a quiet house, the inside is, but outside is all kinds of
noises. (more for example, than at the cuban village.) [*At New York*

World's Fair in 1939; a favorite hangout of Merton and Lax.] more than
in hong kong, shanghai & new york city all put together. i may
move again. i may go to patmos. or to one called astypalea, where
they don't make quite so much noise.

(i'm getting so i really like it quiet.) but all the places it's quiet,
they don't have any water or any food. as soon as there's food &
water, along comes noise.

a man in down-town kalymnos has just invented television; he
just kept rubbing two antennae together & all of a sudden what do
you think he had? visible radio.

so maybe i will go to patmos. (will leave my books in a box
somewhere) & go to wherever it seems ok.

how are you? i don't hear nothing for weeks; did you get my
letter? all my letters (from anywhere) come opened. it is part of the
century's unrest.

i read the books of mircea eliade. he is the best since leo
edwards, the author of the poppy ott series. he has got me wearing
a black ramskin & beating the drums night & day. perhaps this is
what has gotten the natives started.

his books are written first as card-files in roumanian; then
translated into french, from french into german, & from german
(with breathtaking ease) into english. (if you want to understand
what he's saying, you have to go back to the card-files.) but i'm all
for old eliade. he's got all the right ideas.

write me if you can; or send a note by chipmunk. am waiting
your news.

yrs,
Sam

XIII. THOMAS MERTON   *June sevens. 66*

Dear Jope
I don't know if it is the sevens the eights or the nines of june
but it come today your fitful notes. Yes it is the weather. Here the
Yugoslavs are making also the weather, rains of blood, buckets of
piss poured out from airplanes etc. most inhumane fallout all over
the place everybody with dropping out teeth, eyes retreating out
through the backs of the head we are in a state of crisis you better
remain in Greece pal.

Gloom talk about gloom it has taken away the steeple it has destroyed inside the abbey Church, really you would not recognize the old dump. It is nothing but weltschmerz inside and out. Cleverly distilled weldschmerz painless and insidious which sneaks in through new liturgies, tourist guitars, speeches of pontiffs, protestant wits, old black Joe (again) and many others too numerous to mention. I resist the weltschmerz with secret rum and other pursuits. I have against the weltschmerz that it schmerzes too much the whole dam welt, and for this it should be impeached. Let joyous Greece shake it all off, there is still plenty of room for joy at least in Greece. Tell them about this in the Plaza, tell all the boys and the octopus fishery and the pearl hats and the musics in the tavern, tell them to hell with all the Yugoslav insidious weltschmerz and calm down boys and have another round on the house etc like the old days in Lindy's or wherever it was they never gave us no more rounds on the house.

I refuse to be schmerzed by weltschmerz. I resist the schmerz with oaths, with catcalls, with boos, with weak indefinite handsprings since the back is not yet in shape for full leaping hops and wide angle springs. I am in no touch with anybody anymore. I have given up except business I have given it all up except business and love. With Seymour I have no more contacts than with the man in the moon, except I write to old Harpers mag and Old Harpers mag gets on the phone to old Fortune and there is old Seymour nesting behind the encyclopedias writing for fortune and saying haarrrrh. For Harpers mag I have now a pretty small love affair which results in printing a crazy article about the beards of atheists should be made into nests for unreason and presented to the Society of Jesus to be set aflame in brandy. It is a new twist in the ecumenical movement. I am for down with all ecumenicals and up with the Jesuit beards. Let everybody be more sly like in the old days say I. Meanwhile I resist everything and everybody. I am entrenched in the hermit hutch with a small gun and today I shot (at) two dogs which run away chastened (this gun is not a gun to kill you understand it is a small gun to stimulate and to excite, to set in motion and to propel, to urge to withdraw and to compel to vamoose the hell out of my territory to sting up their dam dog tails and get them OUT). (It works.)

Presently the bell rings and everybody got to stop breathing. I continue. The Pakistanis have got Bramachari in a large keg and he will never be let out still less will he ever walk the waters to the USA. I have renounced all thought of Bramachari. Wherever you move you got to take into account the troubles. Down low is lowdown troubles. Higher up is Higher troubles. On top is the highest trouble which is the top of the morning white boss. You tell that man to go to Patmos and invent his TV there. You are right about Mircea Eliade I am all for being a shaman but first my back has got to improve. Also I got bursitis which means a purse on the elbow and damn that purse says I. Well, all I can say is if they got bursitis in Greece you better skip it man. Bursitis is a purse of small hell affixed to the joints and which makes the writings of novel to be sheer roaring grief my curses can be heard from here to Nashville. Does not much good to the novel which is in any case imaginary.

Hey I think you should have got a big package of litanies, lamentations, apocalypses, denunciations, broadsides and TV scripts that I sent by camel last month. Or didn't I? I must of. When I was in the infirmary I sure must of? What did I do when I was in that place except send out piles of crap like that all over the face of the earth to everyone. I must of. When I was in the infirm house it was discovered that I had loss of appetite and they was for a while giving me twenty five year old bourbon for to recover the appetite little did they know that this was the way for me to have no appetite permanent like as long as there lasted the twenty five year old bourbon but it is all now drained the bourbon and I still have no appetite. Phaugh on the appetite. It must be either business or love has destroyed the appetite.

Slate is at the age for the heart's attack. So am I. But I plan first to be struck by lightning from going to walk in thunderstorms. I snap the fingers at life. Well it is getting late and I must let out those dam baboons again.

Release Tom Mooney.

Up the rebels.

Yrs

Dr Livingtsone.

most cherished albert houdini,

the cookies is arrived every one & with each the weights & fortunes. here is a fortune that says help & here is another, sustainment. the ropes are there the pulleys as well: one must only pull on the pulleys & rise on the ropes.

i am sit in my cell all day. all around the cell is hong kong: dancings & clappings. the very trees snap their fingers & the neighbors howl with delight. here in the cell is quies. i think up sketches for the elks club banquet.

who was that psychicos i seen you outwit? (interruption: an old lady—80 years old—climbs a fig tree in my beholding—with a stick—& knocks down a whole bunch of figs) music & dancings continue. this is no psychicos this is barba charlie of the horsemarines. & who was that pneumaticos? this is canon sotiri out of belgio. a small boy (really) climbs the fig-tree & joins his grandmother in the branches.

(the figs are not ripe but the hens can eat them; whatever the hens can eat is worth knocking down.)

this is only the old lady's story: the figs are ripe—she will sit in her cave & eat them.

i sit in my sel— where the quiet is & wait for some ultimate confrontation.

old lady in the tree explains to one on the ground, not how she happens to have climbed a tree, but how she happens to have climbed one not her own.

the small boy is down. he carries a basket. the old lady is down too. there is no task left her but to jump off the high stone fence.

(she crosses her self in gratitude for the catch of figs & disappears into the casbah.)

no more of those scenes. we have our own things to do. reeds & baskets. the hours of the day.

i am reading the messages one by one. each one an extremely splendid message. each one a timely arriver. most of the messages i get these days contain only questions, whereas these both questions & answers.

here is my song for daniel-rops:
                    hoo-ray
                    for
                    ops
                    hoo-
                    ray
                    for
                    ops
                    hoo-
                    ray
                    for
                    hen-
                    ri
                    dan-
                    i-
                    el
                    rops
                    his
                    moth-
                    er
                    was
                    a
                    dan-
                    i-
                    el
                    but
                    she
                    mar-
                    ri-
                    'd
                    a
                    rops
                    hoo-
                    ray
                    for
                    hen-
                    ri
                    dan-
                    i-
                    el
                    rops
                    -

this is a curtain-song for the elk jamboree. (am working up another for mr. g-lagrange at the masons.)

about old ladies: i read another russian release about one who lived to be 157 (on grass & yoghourt); it said "at the age of 137, her dream came true": she was given permission to move from armenia to the ukraine.

much to be learned in the quiet of the cell. i hope you have a quiet cell & reasonable sustenance. (the world is all topsy-turny upside down.) there are only a few cells left.

will write again soon with a stronger pencil.

all the best from the diaspora.

Barnacle Joe Frobenius

XIV. THOMAS MERTON   *July 15. 1966*

Revered Postum:

Yours of the 10th resting in Athens has arrived and I take note of the "restante" and the Athens, not to forget the all important Potsie or Poastie. It is most important that the Poste is stabilized in one place of "restante" and not for example "vagabonde." Thus the letter hath a stable hope of arrival, a sure home, a safe harbor, a place of reste.

Now you are with the film. [*Lax acted in a Greek-American film produced in Athens in 1966 but never released for distribution.*] Ahah, I knew all along you were with the film. As to the script, pay no attention whatever that there is no script. It is always the way today and tomorrow there is no script. In the past there was always a script nine miles long with sanity clauses which the Marx bros had to rip out piece by piece. It was too long all the scripts in the old days. But now all is changed, The audience must make up its own script. You don't have to worry none about nothing. Just show the monks of meteora knocking off their derbies with custard pies and go "POW" on the screen once in a while. That is all the script you need I am telling you. Let the audience do the rest. Audience yell ZOWIE for instance and start knocking off each others derbies right there in the cinema or the restaurant as the case may be.

Headless director. How true. How true. All directors have lost the head writing POW all over the script. You wear the white hat. Beware. The script calls for a crafty monk to sneak up and knock it off with a custard pie? ZOWIE. The movies is full of pep once again, no script just ACTION. If someone yells ACT you jump right in the director's lap. Though if he is a Greek be careful.

No Greeks understand the sportsman.

It is the happy new years of the bursitis. A purse on Toscanini for winning always the Met. That was his trouble. Winning the Met. With a POW and a ZONK while the custards flew by in the air. BONG. Just to make sure you know I aint fooled about how he got that purse. What they done is stick me with painful and rasping cortisone which have the bad kickback eight hours later POW I hit the ceiling ZOWIE and no script needed for that one either BONG. Just to let you know we got all the movie noises right here in the hammocks.

The purses see from the cortisone that the drs mean biz and went away no need massive doses of Vitamin C.KLONG.

You have been in Meteora and you have left with the white derby of sport. Here it is one hundred degrees always and soon I creep down to the monkhouse for a shower there is no other way. I sneer at the purse I have won no Met and yet I have the purse. I have now the sprained ankle. I am all tore up in the joints. I am a veritable orthopedic case rent limb from limb by the drs. They revealed to me they found more dam disk. I tell them forget the disks brother, stick to that cortisone for the old purse and fly in the face of providence as regards the disk. Nuts on the disk is what I privately say I will just lie abed and meditate is what I aver. Watch me. I got a new Buddhist meditation book all about bare attention and clear comprehensions and all the works I learn to float. What does a growing boy care for disks and bumps if he can float, tell me that?

Do not become conscripted by the hairy monks of Meteora.

Be not involved with the old monks of Athos and the falling down monastelly.

Slate wrote a bit in Atlantic monthly razzing the hospitals all about how they give the enema to the visitor instead of the patient (POW and like that). I wrote Slate he must abandon law or be lost. Artic in Atlamphus was very funny like old days with two Slate drawings also. Now I don't have it I gave it away to the medical profession with a dry snarl.

Here everything is hot like a fournaise. I go down to the station to get a Turkish bath and wind up the dam purse. As for you, watch the white hat and be of good cheer. You will see about those mountains if it is cold or hot. ZOOOOM.

    Yr pal

    Cassidy.

XV. THOMAS MERTON   *July 25, 1966*

Dear Prestone:

If you do not have a script for your movies I will write one in fact many. How you met Prince Hotchkiss in the orangerie and discovered that *you* were yourself Prince Hotchkiss. Etc. It shall be called THE HORRENDOUS SURPRISE. A catchy title just for our modern teen age generation which is all agog for catchy surprises don't you think? It is my impression my dear Prestone that we of the Ecclesia must sharpen our wiles to attract the new wave or the teen generation, so artfully called the pepsi generation. For this we must appeal to their disordered imaginations, and that is what I believe your movie ought to be doing right now to *bring the new wave back into the pews*. It is just a question of attracting them back with trinkets so just make sure you have plenty of trinkets in the script. You will start a tidal wave of trinkets in the pews and the new wave will go right on out through the back of the Church washing away the sacristy as it goes. Leaving LSD tablets for the older and more staid generations to scramble for among the wreckage.

No, it is no joke, we must *win the teens*. Or else we are sunk my dear Bish. The chanceries must fold and the curiales must crawl away under the rug if we fail to win the teens. It is the greatest crisis of the moment. Buckets of trinkets and this alone will win teens says Bishop.

Tell the director all I have said and he will bring the pepsi generation back into the pews with all their pepsi bottles full of LSD.

It is your beard that will pack the pews with teens. Never forget this for an instant.

As for the white hat, not so hot, it doesn't CONNECT.

Tell the director what I said.

As for the poems it is self explanatory. It is a laud. It is a serene and profound salute from the alumni. [*See appendix*] It is to be sung with trumpets on deans day every year until kingdom come.

Here the house is very hot and full of animals.

I will not push this tirade any further until you have met Hotchkiss.

Tell the director not to tear down the orangerie but to fill it with pews for the teens. Unrealistic? Maybe. But we must TRY EVERYTHING.

One thing you got to watch in the movie: MUMBLING DICTION. None of that, Prestone, none of that. Must produce 'more pear shaped vowels when saying "C-o-o-o-o-l-d in the mountains." (Cozy the moutons) (Contrast—a trick for teens. Get them in the pews with sly tricks like that.)

Interject an occasional song: "I'm just wild about Harry" (for teens again. Will drive their imaginations wild for pepsi.) (everything they hear they think it is pepsi that is why we oldsters have smartly called them the pepsi generation.) They appreciate being appreciated. Gets them into the pews all in a hugger mugger at the twelve oclock mass at St Birgdigs. It will also help win appreciation if once in a while you yell Beat Rutgers. Just a few words of advice from an old moviegoer.

Yr rich uncle
Moon Mullins.

XVI. THOMAS MERTON   *Aug. 12, 1966*

Hoy:

While you sleep, while all Athens sleeps, Miss Velma [F] does not sleep. She is awake and fathoming the teen age mind. She is packing them into the pews next to the giraffe and the ape. I leave you to judge for yourself about the teen age giraffe. It works. Now to other biz.

In magic Japan you should write to Cid Corman, who edits Origin. He is like at a long fictitious address which I put down with scrupulous cares:

Cid Corman- Origin
Utano, Fukuoji- cho, 82
Ukyo-ku, Kyoto.

The rest is the mystery of the east and the sacred books and the tea leaves etc. You write and ask about you get Origin which sometimes he was giving away for free but very good magazine very good guy I think and writes letters and so on. You can send him yr bks anyhow. I got a sore arm. I don't write no books with a sore arm. I just struggle through writing an article, but it is not worth it with the arm in a burse. If I was Miss Velma I would not be able to pack in the teens because my arm in the burse would make it impossible to tame that giraffe. Such is the melancholy of age.

Here if you wish to make a hit with the clergy all you got to do is stand up and say God is dead and you will be an immediate success. Thus you never heard such a rush of people running and falling over each other to say God is dead. Norman Vincent Peale etc is all God is dead, and positive thinking killed him. The kids in California now got license stickers (true) saying God is not dead he is alive and hiding in Argentina. But as for me I stick to that old home town religion: spell it out with opium. I am the people so why confuse the issue? I want the opium of the people.

You wait I will make a comeback and tame the giraffe.

My arm just dropped off and walked away by itself into the woods. Before I tame the giraffe I got to catch that arm and put it back on and tame it.

Thus I cease from the impromptu compositions and go hold my arm in the sun. Give my regards to show biz.

XVII. ROBERT LAX   *Kalymnos*

Dear Dr. Klaventook,

Miss Velma keeps me awake night & day with her questions. I'd have written long before but it is always Miss Velma with a question: what am I made for? Where is we all going? You are going to Fukuoji-cho, Kyoto. You are going there tomorrow. Never mind the other questions & never mind about the giraffe. You are going to Kyoto on the morning train tomorrow.

And everything else I have is going to Kyoto, too. One thing at a time. One verse at a time. Kyoto is the place. The Japanese are harbingers of good.

It's been a long, hard couple of seasons, I'll tell you. First the films, as I told you, then the visitors, later the krankenhaus (auf Athen). The stomach pump, the rheumatic pains in every conceivable joint. They are drifting away. I'll be well again soon, with the help of St. Dominic Savio.

Miss Velma was first all answers, & then in a sudden turn-about, all questions. Why am I dressed as a clown? Why am I leading a giraffe? How do I come to appear on Radio Kiev? (There was no way at all of apprising her of the facts.)

The fact is, she *wanted* to dress as a clown, she *wanted* to ride a giraffe, she *wanted* to call her sermon that day: "The Circus of Youth"—and all the rest. Well, there she is on her way to Kyoto, & I hope she finds it rewarding.

Here is a couple of longevity stories—the one about Grandma Azmar I've been carrying in my hat for a year. Grandma Azmar has the right idea. She "feels fine." We should all try to feel fine, & not just once a year, but always.

I hope your arm is come back from the woods. (I was wishing only last week my ribs would go there.) It is all right now. They can stay where they are. Am thinking (a little) of moving the whole thing to Patmos.

The whole show, that is. And with all best regards from us all.

Major's Midgets

XVIII. THOMAS MERTON   *Oct. 8*

Dear Major:

At last it has come the scripts of your ult. I note with concerns every sidelong reference to the hospitals. Let us both equally in concert spit on the krankenhaus and stay far from its portals. Let us participate in avoiding the lazaretto, whether in Aten or in Lusvil. Must all avoid the fates and stay quiet in the Kalymnips. Yes it is the exhausting of visitors also everyplace puts jack and jill in the hospital. Furthermore however my suggestion is also to thoroughly avoid Fukuoji ko except to send the snippets and the

snappets and the verses and prosaics but otherwise I think fukuoji ko is a stuffy old hothouse. But doubtless the Japanese are harbingers of good. I would think twice before you was to pack up and go. All time tea ceremonies etc, harbinger of the backache. One verse at a time that is altogether different. Spin them out clockwise week by week that is true prudence. Furthermore as everybody knows the Luganoes have gone busted, have been taken over by the banks, have been settled in the banqueroute. Most tiresome for the Luganoes. And for all the fellows. No more luscious twenty page offprints etc. To replace the offpramps of Lucky Lugano is perhaps to snoop around and find other primts.

Now you will notice that while you slept Miss Velma has got way out in front. She is now out in front of the entire human race. She has passed everybody by. She has shaken off the dust of her feet alike on Beatle and B. Graham. She is the nonpareil of wig and guitar. Next week she will doubtless win as a bear. Yes she will indeed pack them in as polar bear, yes indeed she will. As polar bear. No wonder she changes all the times from answers to questions and from questions back to answers. It is to outwit the concurrences that she has done this.

Yes you are perfectly right that Miss V. has been wilful about the giraffe but it can't be helped. She is not to be stopped from anything, and no degree of wilfulness baffles her ingenuity. She is on the way to Kyoto to test her wilfulness on the easterns. She will soon find out they will be putty in her hands. That is what she wanted all the time, putty.

The story of Gramma Azmar is written entirely by dupes. She does not feel fine. She is the dupe of the commissars. She has been drugged in radio Kiev with sunflower seeds. Azmar is the Russian for asthma. She is really a dupe who is suffering from asthma as a result of trying to bug the offices of American consuls and putting sunflower seeds in the samovars of the CIA. Thus it always was with the dupes. Do not be duped with the duped clergy. Grandma Azmar is an impostor aged ten and a half do not be fooled by her asthma. Also when she was in Turkey she preferred it to Armenia as is well known from her oblique statements on Radio Kiev. She wrote insulting notes to the president of Armenia on the backs of sunflower seeds. It is in this way that she first became a dupe. But Miss Velma is no dupe. She is the genuine goods. The old man who did not inherit two million dollars was no dupe. He was ninety four years old and he knew it. How many of our younger generation can say the same? Only Miss Velma.

Never did hear from old slate. Everyday go in the woods to look for myself a wooden arm. Will send packs of luckies and goodies to dupe Kalymnos.

XIX. ROBERT LAX

Most dear Captain,

am in fastest receipt of yours of the inst. both of the edifying cables, the notes on the world and latest news of captress Velma. all of these are arrived just in time to save the lives of the many. the many have assembled in the public square for ovation.

i too am in the public square, but my foot is in a sling, or plaster hammock. the hammock is come from athens to keep my foot in it for the nurse (the dunce, the nouns). my foot is in a plaster cast because of the rheums and arthurs. (the rheums and arthurs are enemies of the doctor & this is why. doctor promises however, only one week in the plaster cast & after that, all dancings.) i will let you know about the dancings the minute they begin.

(this all comes from the causes we have mentioned. the causes we have mentioned are the veritable causes. the minute we see the hat of a visitant appearing over the hillside, that is the time to take up our cudgeons.)

now to the cables [*"Edifying Cables," an early version of* Cables to the Ace]: of all the cables, these, the edifying are the most exalting of all. i read them & read them & again in the morning i will read them. very crazy cables, deeply moving every one, & the whole together as a poem. there should be thousands more such cables. the world should be full of such cables. language is a medium as you have rightly invented. it is a medium like any other. like sulphur, for example & bernstein. these are the mediums who operate in every part of the world. not so, these editfying cables. they have cleared the air of all media.

have also read your attack on albert camels;but have not yet finished. i do not know how will it all come out. was he buried, as i have heard once, in a wimple of the benedictions?

---

then too i am in receipt of many koans & satoris. i keep the prettier one for myself & give the other to a girl you would have wanted me to. (she is 17; she makes pencil jane o'malley & all the girls in bradford look like a snub.) she is gone away to a new satori. i sit in the cave & heat up the water again for some more mountain tea.

no, sir, no tokio. no tokio joe for jack. very gloomy part of the world i'm sure. i'll send them my haikus one by one. but now let us turn to Miss Velma.

oh, ho, ho. here is yet another visitraps. quick, to the door. quick, the curmudgeons. i will wire you anon.

Captain Muckridge

HERE IT IS ALL ABOUT THE MORNING THAT LITTLE TRACY LITTLEFIELD WAS EATEN UP BY MISTAKE BY MRS. ROSEN - Vinalhaven

(from a newspaper)

Birthday Surprise

Mrs. Marion Littlefield was pleasantly surprised Wednesday morning when several of her friends dropped in for coffee in honor of her birthday. The surprise was planned and given by her daughter-in-law, Mrs. Betty Littlefield with whom she makes her home.

Those present were Mrs. Fred Geary of Fulton, New York, Mrs. Richard Geary daughter Betsy, Mrs. Fabian Rosen, Mrs. Hilma Webster, Mrs. Hazel Roberts and little Tracy Littlefield, her granddaughter. Mrs. Mary Olsen was unable to attend.

MRS OLSEN KNEW WHAT SHE WAS DOING

Cadette Girl Scouts Meet in Owls Head

OWLS HEAD—The first fall meeting of Cadette Girl Scout Troop 559, was held October 10 at the home of the leader, Mrs. Vera Mathieson. Ruth Doty was elected troop treasurer and Gail Lindsey troop scribe. Patrol leaders are Deborah Orne, patrol 1 and Brenda Stone patrol 2.

Other members of patrol 1 are Cheryl Iott, assistant patrol leader; Nancy Mathieson, Gail Lindsey and Sharon Iott. Other members of the second patrol are Rebecca Hary, assistant; Ann

Mathieson, Ruth Doty and Kathy Orne. The troop also elected Nancy Mathieson and Kathy Orne to be delegates for the troop at various meetings. The first meeting will be held at Watts Hall, Thomaston, on Oct 21, after school.

It was decided the refreshment "Cookie Box" will be brought to each meeting by troop members in alphabetical order. Ruth Doty will bring the box at the next meeting.

Girls will work on badges in connection with the Challenge of Emergency Preparedness, and will include "Campcraft," "Family Camper," "First Aid," "Games," "Hiker" and "Pioneer."

Slow Down and Live

Everything was going all right here till Rebecca Hary bucked at the part about "Slow down & live." She was followed in this move by Cheryl Iott & Kathy Orne, all of whom then left "The Cookie Box" to Ruth Doty.

XX. ROBERT LAX   *Kalymnos*
                                                     3 noembrio

Dear Colonel Hoopsaboy,

here we are again, straignt from the clysters & half as good as new. each day brings to light new wonders of science, today's wonder is they have taken off the plaster & give me back my foot. the foot does not yet dance, but even that it should walk along is a wonder of science. (the dancing is soon: we will play it some music.)

as to Miss Velma, she has won the race. she has won it hands down. she has won it hands & feet down. she has brought them back to the pews. they are stumbling back into the pews right now while Miss Velma plays the guitar. she is the beatle woman of youth: youth is climbing over itself & into the pews for Miss Selma. the pews are all full of Martians. they are stamping out the rhythms of Miss Velma in the pews. she has thought of the simplest of formulas: pure sex & beauty, & has won the race. perhaps that is not the formula at all; but she has won. the trophy goes to Miss Velma & to no other wight.

i was thinking anyway we should write her a letter: not you,

---

not i; but dimitri haracoupolos, a friend of mine on the islands. i was thinking we should suggest a hundred or so new costumes & approaches, in case she should run out of any. but Miss Velma will never run out. she is a winner from the word bang, go! she will win with the wig; she will win without the wig. she will conquer the bastinados of the orient. she will march them captive with herself in the lead down beverly & alvarado: you will see.

now to our other projects. i have not sent a single haiku to kyoto, but i will. i will stay away from the orient otherwise. & i will stay away from all old ladies like Granny Azmar. they are dupes. she is a dupe of the armenians. will stay away from most armenians too. (this is all a part of the orient.) i will stay where i am in kalimpsest & wait.

i never hear from slate either, though i write a cajoling note every Christmas to himself & his wife. they never send any jokes in return. this has gone on for several years, though they took me to the train when i left, & told me to come back. he only writes to William Lyon Phelps. he never writes to his poor old college buddy-roops.

reinhardt does. every once in a while he puts on his old raccoon coat & looks up his friends. & rice has taken to wearing his psi u button night & day. i never can forget the old days myself, with old dean mcknight & the rest. & griselda & murray sylvester & camille.

i will have to go out & chop some wood pretty soon. i will put the wood around my foot & tell it tanz. foot is really quite alright but not yet dancing. soon we will try. it is a miracle of silence. moonlights in rio. blume from hawaii. der graf von luxemburg. what ever querschnitte of music comes into the orchestra's fifteen heads. everyone in the rhythmus studio: tvist, tvist, tvist, tvist.

write soon when you can & give our best to all the monk-brothers when you see them. rice will be coming through the midwest on his way to armenia, it looks like. you shld tell him hello.

yrs,
Sam

here is all the lucky numbers on your hit parade, including a mystery tune you can never identify. [*List from a German catalog of musical tape recordings.*]

Operetten-Querschnitte
(19 cm/sec — 30 Minuten)
Nr. 53 Der Graf von Luxemburg (Léhar)
Nr. 54 Die lustige Witwe (Léhar)
Nr. 55 Paganini (Léhar)
Nr. 56 Blume von Hawaii (Abraham)
Nr. 57 Viktoria und ihr Husar (Abraham)

Nr. 25 Moonlights in Rio
Nr. 26 Slow time
Nr. 27 Jazz in Stereo
Nr. 28 Tanz mit mir
Nr. 29 Twist everybody Twist
Nr. 30 Rhythmus Studio 17

XXI. ROBERT LAX   *Kalymnos*
                                                  december 5 66

Dear Ambassador Philbrick,
   a lot of snow has gone under the chipmunk since my last
flash. i am once again in kalimpops. we have wrapped aunt zelma
into the flag & hoisted her off with a whoopsaboy. she will
entertain our troops on venus, & that is the last of that one.
   velma is different: trudging in & out of chicamunga boulevard
in an endless series of hats. we will return to her in a minute.
   i have been in & out of athens as many times as the turks:
there is nothing to be seen there, nothing, nothing. my foot is out
of the hammock; science has triumphed. still i prefer to hop along
on the other. as to burse & no nurse, i have this to say: a canadian
redskin of my acquaintance had the burse most painful but says
the doctors found a drug or sovereign herb that cured it. shall i
write & ask him what is the name of the herb?
   have had many visitors & more on the way. friends of howard
gold; friends of padre tomas; howard gold, himself; &, as i think,
padre tomas. these friends of howard gold's have come to stay. we
have found them a house on another side of the island.
   i am living, starting today, in two houses: one cold palace in
the downtown section & one warm hutch on the hill. i will start

moving into the hutch, but slowly, slowly.

maritain: you are right—they used to make people then. i am glad he come out & see you. you must send me a velox of those you have taken.

as to the alchemy club at verazzano high school, you are right there, absolutely. let others play on the school magazine: we will stick to the sulphurs & antinomy. (thos. mann himself was a pontifex asinorum who could never be replaced by albert camels or the nuns.)

miss velma, as you may have heard, has taken over the entire field of literature. every last pamphlet. every pink & blue throwaway. every octavo; every duodecimo. sears & roebuck buys the encyclopedia britannica; cbs buys random house; random house buys alfred knopf. herder & herder belongs to the a & p. (you open an octavo of spiritual reading, it is all full of fish sticks & frozen horse-meat.)

i hardly admire anything these days but the ancient chinese. but you must explain to me about zen archery. (i got it all clear about the tea, now: just the archery.) it isn't that you shouldn't aim at the target, it's that you shouldn't shoot for a prize. or is it that you shouldn't shoot for a prize, but aim at the target? or which? am out every day with my book & the arrows, but all i am hitting at all is postman & neighbors.

gas heater: i will get a gas heater, too. perhaps if i had a gas heater i wouldn't move from house to house as i do to keep warm. one gas heater, one house & that is all.

once again i am happy with the edifying cables. these are the most superior kind of poem. it takes considerable reading & rereading to understand the sense of them. but now at last i understand the sense of them: am able to convey their meanings in every direction.

a happy Christmas to you & the boys in the north. it is doubtful that any cards will go out from here (not even from the department of hams & cheeses) none. will sit on a rock by the sea all Christmas day, thinking, thinking, thinking.

will think & think of the old days: naomi this & old bruce that. i will think until they carry me into the house.

all the best to brother tiger. get well & write us soon again.

yours,

Sam

My Dear Upsurge:

Do not give it even a wink, merely testing the types, merely proving the provo, approving the inapprobabile, and reproving the innocence machine. This morning in the colds of Jans I was wyping the article and wiping the follicle and hunting the comical with verve and rage with the types skipping right and left, no caps and no flaps, no bumps and too many stumps, all over the root was hairs of the hat in a commando of mishaps. Now I have wipe the noses of the tpyes and everything flies right and left with much skills except for the fingaroo of the typer which is drunk with rheums and aged with brusk burses. So now it makes the caps and flips the flaps and puts the hats on every commando. This is all I required to know, but having started the epistola is it not meet to finish with a marathon? It is truly says the Ptolemies and the Protos of Athos and the Athos or Aramis and the Dartigan partigan or the Irish martinet of Dumaze.

Do not give it even a spink or a clink as I walk in my cangue and flap my cuffs at the toughs and the cops car tethered all at once to the half of a star and the end of a flying saucy.

O the saucy the saucy little muss whup from Mars is come down the chimbley with Santa under the suit and with an old salt in the camp. Crumple up the saltines for Santa he will be wan if you do not. Santa has went in a foam these two weeks back leaving only pictures of Seymour's Julia and her horse. I write some day to Seymour about his Julia [*Freedgood's daughter*] and her horse. Did you get the Julia and the flying saucy?

It is woods in a fallow and birds in the holler with Faulkner riding a train around my room every morning. This is the spirits of my trump ace as I sit and think in the silences to write me a book of Old Doc Falkner and his uncle Major who won the south with pankakes [*spelling reflects difficulty with typewriter*] and his bottle. Uncle has the clan in his kitchen and all the darkies humming and strumming and old man Ribber droolling in his droll bib and aunt in the case and uncle in the wasp nest with that fool Camptown. Get back in your chair its all right they aint coming in at the window like you think, it is only a passing show.

Like the aark and the saucy is coming by one evening with lights lit and domes unfolded and flowers coming out at every eye

to the tones of untoward music. Maritain is there with Skakspur and Homaire and the poet Lothaire and the windy air and all the musics with the longest hair is drawn the saucy down from Mars out there so far so far it is lyric how far they were.

We now introduce the parade of the old past fallen year with his barba in the soups of Xmas which has chilled in the interim from neglect of the viewer. Santa was there but failed.

Hop skip and an old jomp as Johnson Pres flies over the fence in a wheelbarrow. He is in with the VN commandos he is into the China question burrowing around with his anteaters on every side and he will find it full of more ants than you would ever think. And who killed Robin Kennedy that old turtle dove he cried in the mawnin with his nose in the China question like he was full of the ants. But it turned out to be a good question.

Let the upbringing of the Greeks be always surging toward Eureka and the Emporium and the Emporheben and the heaving up of mighty fine new years says old Joe Plain in the top of the morning pinnacle of Patrick Harbor. Plain as day is the time of Patrick yet two month away in the silly shambles of old Blarney Google. With mushrawms and leprechaums and the chums of the humdrum bullet. But it turned out to be a good old Irish question all right and the nose of the question was so dam full of ants that he sneezed all over the country.

Once upon a time there was a country. It was called William Faulkner and it was the power of the southern railway train and amen amen amenamen.

Beg another amen for benaben and bene volente and ben hubbard [*director of extra curricular activities at Columbia when Merton and Lax were there*] in the woods with ken and eagle and click and zick and zeke and eke and ike and the bike. Benaben is under the mother hubbard with the wife of an old wen.

I think this ought to be enough to teach me to quit and get back into the beds of the workaday zen. Let every good man return to the party and the fox retire from the old black dog of lazy joe. It is the end of the test and the test was a shining success. Give Velma a big hug.

Nunkle.

Holloy:

Here is Towser conducting the symphony. [*Picture
accompanying ad for doctor's guaranteed method of dog-training.*]
Without force or threat, he never threatens his master's voice, he
never snarls and snaps like dogs not well trained. He appreciated
natural reflex. He was humane. He is humane. He conducts the
symphony of man. That is the secret. The symphony of man is
more jolly when conducted by Towser without humane threats
whips or dog medicines.

Your dog wants to be trained by Dr Towser Whitney: he loves
the method. That is the trouble with most people, they don't love
the method. All the people should learn from Towser.

How to start it says without even touching Towser. Not only
lay aside the whip but Towser must understand that you have not
even a hostile thought, not even an umbrage. There is in the mind
not even the first movements of a thought that Towser is inferior.
The mind does not even twitch at Towser. Life is full of enjoyment.
The training has already begun. Towser has trained you and you
never knew it.

This is the secret: THINK DOG.

He will stop himself from table leg chewing. That is all right.
But how to stop Uncle Horace from table leg chewing. Ah. That is
different.

CURE SHYNESS. He thinks bold. Even among strangers. Arf
Arf Arf. See the strangers fly in all directions. Shyness rapidly
cured. Sure fire.

Knows now 400 words. But what words? You must
immediately cross out at least 100 words he picked up from Uncle
Horace.

WITH FOUR HUNDRED WORDS YOU CAN WRITE A
MASTERPIECE (Lohengrin for example).

Towser is of course now admittedly known to be the author of
Lohengrin. He 'fessed up!

"IT IS I WHO WROTE LOHENGRIN I GRAF TOWSER." One
of the words he learned is in German ("Graf"=That is his name).

What is he conducting? He is conducting Graf.

HE CAN SHAKE HANDS WITH A LADDER AND SO CAN
YOU. But you must first try. All the world must come and learn

optimism from Towser. Ten days and he paid nothing. You too can pay ten days of nothing with Graf Towser, but learn optimism. It is the "in" lesson: (optimism).

Put away the whip. There is no longer any need.

Shake old Mao Tse Tung and tell him: "Put away the whip, Graf Towser says it can't work. You can't win with the whip."

In the end it is always the same: "Even an childs can done it."

Childs restaurant of course, the place where Towser had to be house broken or else.

I dare you to better Towser. Look at him again. Was there ever such a well-pleased young scholar? He admitted he liked the method. Few have the courage and good sense to do as much.

Well, I got to get the ice off'n my nose and say my office. Guess who was here yesterday? Jonathan Williams, yessir. [*North Carolina poet, publisher, and cross-country hiker.*] With his coat and his cap and his printing press and the three kings all from Lexington.

XXIV. ROBERT LAX   *Kalaboose jan 18 1 9 6 7*

Dear Captain Hopscotch,

have been running around with all those bent arrows in my crown, but am feeling better now since the migrans left, & hope you the same. here is a song (now where is that song) that miss velma wrote just before she was shunted off to the kalaboose. (accused of being a professional do-gooder she denies (her eyes athwart with the fabrication) that she is either professional or d-g. court rules this out & she is off, without further appeal, to the cell-blocks.) she is known now as the song-bird of the nominalists, or the ism's wild thrush, as you will see from her song (where is it now?). her last & only worth-while contribution to the nom/real debate which we hope is over.

though here she is again as patroness of the arts: a former exotic dancer [*another news story*], it says, she saved her bricks & oil shares and has partly obscured a gauguin with her shoulder. better all this than vice versa. interviewed on the opening night, she said "i have tried to bring all things together good into one small room." cell-block 305, that is, where she sits with a faded octavo of nick carter.

i have been, dear mostwich, in & out of the jumps. yesterday i eat the wrong spinach, am taken with a seizure, am all packed up & ready for the hospice when i run into a druggist instead. he says, no, no, no: go home; lie down, it will all go away. i hope it is the same with your burses. take cortisone, yes: but avoid dr wulf who's friend to man & let no scalpel enter thy copse.

here it is tingling cold (though sure if it tingles here it must klang there). i too must write my letter to the nuns: let every nun make her poems in the coffee house, like sister hilary of the sônes. let every nun take tambourine & banjo & let them pipe upon their reeds. the world is better for it & the nuns no worse.

well, as you say, it turned out to be a very good question. the personal responsibility of every darky on the delta. something our anteater pres will have to work out for himself. he's worked out everything else so good, so far. a matter of deep concern to every numbskull in the noösphere. something he'll have to straighten out for himself.

well, here is the song from miss velma. the end of the realist controversy & the beginning of the lovestonite rebellion. names & things, it is called, & that's what it says.

what happened this year? no mama's orange rings? (ah well, no matter.) mama's in heaven ring'd with rinds.

yrs,
Sam

names	names
&	&
things	things
names	names
&	&
things	things
things	things
&	&
names	names
things	things
&	&
names	names

things	things
&	&
names	names
things	things
&	&
names	names
names	names
&	&
things	things

— — —

XXV. THOMAS MERTON *Jan 26 67*

Dear Flammarion:

Enough of these Bradford Belly Dancers. [*Same story as above. Wife of oilman: exotic dancer and art collector.*] Let them shade the Gauguins no more with their hip. I can tell their exotics all the way from here. And she is one of the more enormous exotics I can tell that. Where was she when we was there? Where was exotica? In the biblioteca. The Belly Dancers have all set the libraries on fire and this is the current state of the cultures, with their pop arts and their cold husbands. Husband in bed with the colds and wife doing the Belly Dance with Gauguin: what will become of the Christian home? I'd like to see her try that HERE. Miss Velma would tell her a thing or two on the golden altar of miracles and them Gauguins. Think of the expense. But that's the way in Greece, it was always so. Influence of the Turks.

If she is in Cell block 305 she is where she belongs but I do not think they can keep her there.

She will be out dancing around with Gauguin painting something on her belly. It is the limit. What is to become of art at this rate?

I am shocked at the state of art when it has come to this.

Think where we would be if only we had bought oil shares.

Consider the exaggerations of the prints. "LOOKING AT FOUR WORKS OF ART." It is a damned lie. She is looking at only one work of art. At the others she is pointing her bodies. Who can say which is the worst? Not me.

But Miss Velma in her poem coming up out of the pythian earth is the oraculur finish of all the nominals. How true: names things, things names, stings and stocks can break my box but names can never affront.

Now my advice is just to avoid the spinach. Lie on the back and avoid the spanish. Evade the jumps. Cottage cheese only. I am living on a beautiful herb called Bio Strath elixir. It is truly the top sovran elixir from Switz all full of Vitamin B edelweiss and clovers. I am living in and with a hot water bottle on the elbows. I am truly spry and full of fun, but am pursued by the vilifications of progressed Catholics. Mark my word man there is no uglier species on the face of earth than progressed Catholics, mean, frivol, ungainly, inarticulate, venomous, and bursting at the seams with progress into the secular cities and the Teilhardian subways. The Ottavianis was bad but these are infinitely worse. You wait and see.

Yep and old anteater prexy is still asking himself that same question. Will he finally discover that he himself is the one?

No orange rings for mama this year. It is always indian summer. My new song is "O How I Hate The Foods." I wish to withdraw decently to a liquid diet but oh who will save for me the right liquids? Here in this hopechest is nothing but vile milks which make me sick. Away with the milks and bring on the bourbons I cry with supreme conviction but who is there around to be convinced?

Nothing to send, no musics, no poems, no statements, no blast-off, only the ikon of WC Fields [*newsphoto of W. C. Fields at billiards*]. If I can find ikons in this mess; hopefully. Watch out for spinach. Eat only hot water bottles.

Yrs.

XXVI. THOMAS MERTON   *Feb 4 67*

Ho:
Look what is come while all Athens slept. Velma she not slept. She was with Rip Van Winthops. She was not slept she was only resting. Now she is back with more subjects than you can boggle the mind at. She is the Batwoman of Youth. This we knew all

along only we were not able to put it into the exact words. She has found the right words and she will make a man out of Robin. She will fly out of the Jail with seven blazing torches. She will dance in the dell. She will pick out of the congregamption all that are to be healed of their woes. This is your chance. Throw away the canes and fly with Velma.

I must get you this message in haste before the great world disaster which is every week in the next hotel to Velma. In one hotel it is all Batman and hope, in the other it is all dumps and world disasters. It takes all kinds to make a world religion.

It is however plain that each Sunday there is to be a gigantic world disaster from now on. Get ready.

Nothing more except to say that great beauties is come from Emil Antonucci, the Sea anemones and the Thoughts, the deep sea thoughts and moons, the delicate high tides.

I will now close with a topical poem of small statures and low degree: as it were a haiko:

> As they drew near
> To the hermitage
> They caught the strains
> Of a fox trot
> Can this be equalled
> Even in Kalymnos?

More about the pistachios later when I got more residues. Enough that Velma is loose again.

XXVII. ROBERT LAX   *Kalymnos Feb 21*

Most dear Feuerbach,

How happy we were to hear the latest—it cannot be the last—of Miss Velma. If now she flies it is only the first giant steps in her aeon-long causeway. If now she descends it is only the beginning of deeper descents from even higher perches. This we know. If now she flies out of the gaol, will she not blaze back again with torches flying? All for youth. Or as she says, for "The Mighty Miracle of the Restoration of Youth!" That sounds more like it. Gives us a better picture, on the whole, of the youths that crowd in for the flyings. (She's not the only Bat Woman in the overflow

---

crowd.) You can be sure of that.

A pox on the rest of the crowd with their world disasters. Miss Velma's got the right idea, & you see whose ad looks nicer, too. Here's her sister, Sister Bugle [*Another newspaper ad.*] Here's her card & diploma. Sister Bugle lays a calming hand on the world's beatled brow. (She doesn't sleep either.) Consultations night & day. Business & pleasure, love & disease. All busses stop in front of her house, unloading the lucky ones who want to ask her questions. They bring a dollar & the diploma. Rocking back & forth in the fumes, she answers. Readings are confidential if so desired, otherwise blabbed up & down Second Avenue to her & your hearts' content. Sister B's not the beagle woman of youth (you can tell it from her sign); still she's a miracle of science & know-how, wisdom & up-to-date methods—results in 3 days—& a solace to the world.

Here also is come the bunch of cookies most handsome from No Directions. I am frapped herein with all I see: from the right, from the left, from every other line of the compass. Your own poems stand out from the others as stars from the great wooly night; & I am struck once again with Seneca as though it were my very cousin. & here is Pessoa, looking good in the prints. He is funny: he leaves a residue(as I told my doctor) in the mind, & takes the poem away. I like his village. I like his bus.

& here is news from Nancy Flagg's mother: she is just print a book called "Camera Adventures Through Africa." Whether she went herself or just sent the camera is hard to tell, but it couldn't have been easy either way.

Yours,
Sam

XXVIII. THOMAS MERTON   *April 5 67*

Dear Hobbs:

All is dizzy with vernals. Flowers spring up in the closets among the coats. Birds nest in the coffee pot. Abbot gone a maying with Mistress Finch. Hermit hideth beer cans in the bush. Saint Goslop puts up the axe and falls into a sigh. Visits come from all sides. Today comes Slate with big legal parcels and we fabricate the laws: new laws for sun and moon, new laws for Mother Nature, new laws for all except the Pentagons which is to itself a monstrous law of its own. Necessity the mother of conventions is making the law for inconvenience and will see to it that China gets out of order.

Meanwhile my dear Topper we will convene old Slate and I and make laws for the old times, laws for the Barbary Coast, laws for the fickle fens of Arcady, by-laws for the 116 St Subway, etc. Saint Subway, pray for us. Saint Turnstile, pray for us. Saint Nickel, do us the alms. Etc. But I hear in the subway is not saints but alas hoodlings. Saint Hoodlings, horray for us. Saint Mavrix, borrow us a car. Saint Baeter, bait us a train. Such is the litanies of spring in the wealds. Saint Wealds, turn us a trick. Saint Willow, cage us a trush. Saint Trush, ride us a rainbow, ETC.

Saint Mixmix, shake us a cocktail. Saint Burrow, borrow a dime. Saint Sassafras, murmur a sound. Saint Uncle Tom, save the race. ETC. Saint Henry Miller, . . . oops.

Saint Wristwatch: preserve the days of the week.

Saint Calendar: sell us machines.

Saint OIL: burn us the engine.

Saint Glue: sniff us the sweets. ETC.

Well, the main points is here the newest pictures of Towser. He is back in school. He has to do third grade all over again because of getting in bad company. Well now here he is back in third grade with Dr Whiskey and MUCH MORE EAGER than before. Look at the eager look. He pleads for wisdoms. What is Dr Whiskey saying? Is he mumbling under his breath "Get the bag? Let's get the hell outa here? etc." God forfend. Saint Forfend: preserve the morale. Dr Whiskey has nothing but good news and Towser is dying for good news. But pal look behind Towser and what does one see? Agents of the underworld, a veritable Mephisto of a cat, and the Dr is perhaps himself a deluded whiskey not realizing he is a Faust. Is Towser fallen into the hands of Faust? Such is next week's question. I got more questions about that belly dancer, for my mind returns quasi automatic to every belly dancer in the universe since it is spring.

Saint Belly: dance us a Gauguin.

There was once a lady with tatooed hips
She planted Bradford Pa all over with tulips
She dances in the Emery's Beamy bar

She danced on the roof of every rich man's car
Chinese lady she dance with the belly
Velly welly, velly welly.
In this instance we have the true origins of Gauguin.
Enough of the piffle. I must work off the beard and go to see
Slate.
Have springs and joys in Kalympops.
Must admit operatio on the bracchio was no damn good didn't wk.

XXIX. ROBERT LAX   *Kalimpops Apr 15 67*

My dear Hemson,
I am just unfolding yours of the unst & here is Towser again.
He is learning you say. But I hasten to tell you most dear Farbish
that Towser only seems to be learning; will never learn. It is the cat
in the corner who learns; has learned & forgotten. This is Dr
Suzuki his cat & not as one might have supposed Mephistopheles
of the operas. It is only that he hisses & steams like the opera. This
is his teabags. He is throwing a fright into Dr Whiskey. (Dr Faustus
meanwhile is on a trip around the world & will soon be back with
his wife (Nora Joyce-Emma Jung-Charlotte Bronte) to straighten out
the whole mess.)
But as you say: look at Towser. Could anyone be more eager?
Could any dog be more eager? He wants to learn everything Dr
Whiskey can impart. And look at Dr. Whiskey: he sits athwart the
ottoman & is a born teacher. Towser will learn: he will learn to
count, to roll over twice & to handle a revolver. But as you know &
as Dr Suzuki his cat very obviously knows, he will never really
learn. Poor Towser. Poor eager weltschmerz.
Take one more look: who does Dr Whiskey look like most?
Our President. Who does Towser look like most? Our people. Who
does the cat look like most, if you look at him close? The great
sprawling land of China. What then is the parable? Towser will
never learn. That's really the whole story.
I suppose by now Saint Turnstile has come & gone. I suppose
by now new laws have been made for Saint Belly. What yopes did
he make in the woods the well-loved Slate?
What new laws have been made for the humming bird (move

it) for the mountain (fall) for the sea (jump ashore) for the fish (sing) for the bird (desist to whistle) for sister mary coritta (put down your shears) for norman laliberté (desist to whistle) natalie kalmus (take up the sledge) nokomi bird-dog (whistle).

philip lamantia (plant potatoes) brother antoninus (draw straight lines) bishop healey (adjust your collar) canon klopstock (drop that flag).

new laws for robert gibney & nancy flagg. new laws for james fitzsimmons & robert paul smith. unbreakable laws for seymour. whole new set of laws for ned. new law for kilburn. new law for pauker. new law for sister wahoo. new laws for milton & melville crane.

(what ever happened to old bill monahan (donahue) donegan who came to the freshman hops & used to drink beers in the west end: maybe even came from douglaston.) what ever happened to him i wonder.

whatever happened to cecil arrowsmith? (rice's friend who heard that the hudson river day-line boat he was on was going down, so went downstairs to his cabin, packed his shirts carefully, came up again & stepped off onto a trawler just in time?)

whatever happened to camille?

camille has bought a lot of gauguins & is standing on her head inside them.

it is orthodox Easter here in a week or so. every orthodox Easter they blow off half of the mountain here with their dynamites. must start rowing now to keep rocks off the head. get well the bracchio. a pox on their so-called efficacious remedies.

Yrs,
Tiger

XXX. ROBERT LAX   *Apr. 25 67*

Dear Uncle Flipper,

Well, we have finally heard from Aunt. Sandor & Vashti have been giving her a lot of trouble & she has finally decided to lock them both in the closet & to sit outside with Grandpa's (you remember Grandpa)'s slingshot to more or less keep them both in place. it is only understandable. Aunt's nerves had been strained to the breaking point, & that is what happened.

Everything else is quite all right. There is something wrong with the radio now—it is down to only one station & only plays music all day long. I am going to Patmos, the isle of the saints for a week or so, & then right back to Kalymnos, where I know my way around.

I have just drink your latest on the terrors of Albert Camels [*Albert Camus*] & find it extremely good. He is my favorite of all the new french authors & your analysis of his thinking process the keenest I ever saw. He would never have died in the habit. This is a fabrication of the ursulines—Albert Camels has the right idea. We must all run the ridges & never lie down in the sumps.

I am always getting letters from my sister in Olean saying hurray for the works of Thomas Mertox: She is always reading your works & always in magnificent agreement & never at all, not once, for old time's sake.

forever,
Sam

XXXI. ROBERT LAX   *Patmos (kalymnos, like Tuesday)*

Fellow Tuaregs,

well you're right, it's kick the fez day now, or anyway it was. little goliath showed big samson that time & no mistake. old nasser laughing on the other side of his throne this time i'll tell you. 100 million arabs must be wrong. the old one-two & disaster averted. everybody loves a winner. nobody loves a disaster. we have to avert disastrers in all parts of the world. the thing is: always get the drop on disaster. don't ever let disaster get the drop on you.

we've been averting a few right here & everyone is the better for it. dancing in the streets again, a country full of thriving city-states. patmos is very quiet. there is only the sound of old ben hubbard walking up & down the halls.

in a few days i may go to kalymnos, from kalymnos maybe to kephalos, from kephalos who-knows, to La Valsainte, & from la valsainte to some franciscans overlooking sienna. but all of that in the dim misty past or future. each of us with the help of his angels is encouraged to avert his own disasters. (keep an eye on fort knox

& the gelatines.)

as to business: hooray for business. correspondence soon to be published in cartas. catch of non letters in invisible inks. 4-day free trial offer. money back before payment. guarantee. also poems dances in chemical journal. vaporization papers. poum issue. zoom issue. annual plam or graduation issue.

makes one glad to be alive in these times, or in fact in any times, or even at all.

this is not entirely a joke (though maybe it is) of la valsainte (visitor's chambers). whenever i think of leaving these goats, this ocean, i wonder for where. not marrakesh: it's fez day. it is, in fact, fez day in all parts of the world.

write, anyway, whenever you do, to kalimpsest.

yrs,
W. Manone

XXXII. THOMAS MERTON   *July 3 '67*

Dear Wingy:

Yes you are right it is fez day all over the place. I have your prints of the ult in which you refer playfully to the front rooms of La Val Sainte. I don't know about that particular box but it seems to me that old Switz is a little more cozy this morning than where you is or was at the presents when you writ. I do not have the info, you understand, the TV tubes is blowout and the transistors is conk, the communicados has all kicked the fez around here but according to my best understanding it is again all full of planes under the same fez and all is warmups and pressups and Nasser is swinging the arms and touching the toes and all them boys is ready to go, what with the Russkis right behind them mayhap. There is many a hap twixt the fez and the cap. My suggestion would be to avoid both and evade the hap and make for the Alp with a lobster feather on your scalp. Or maybe dull Norway or grim Denmark or doleful sverges: all in the dumps friend, no need of a fez in such dumps as these But maybe Switz clocks hath the magic montage. The Matterhorn is the Message and the modiste is the massage and Marshall MacLompoc is Mother Macree. All is interchangeable on account of fez day which tomorrow I celebrate

---

with graham crackers yes billy graham whose modicum is his mistake, whose podium is his passage, whose vaudeville is his vestige. (He got a fez hid under his vest for when it is fez day in the ole southland like tomorrow.)

Every man got to avert his own disaster whether with the fly-swatter or the eggbeater or the hub cap or the radiator. It is an age to technics and potlucks in which the midday is the postage: it is now midday and I haste for the postamt where the melodeon is the moustache.

Heave ho the crumpet and away with
the fez or the fink fuzz.

XXXIII. THOMAS MERTON   *Sept 5 67*

O Lax:

Do you know the great sorrows? Just heard today by clipping from Schwester Therese about Reinhardt. Reinhardt he daid. Reinhardt done in. He die. Last Wednesday he die with the sorrows in the studio. Just said he died in a black picture he daid. The sorrows have said that he has gone into the black picture for he is dead. All I read was the clip. Very small clip. Say Reinhardt was black monk of the pix and he daid. Spell his name wrong and everything. Dead none the less. Tried at first to figure it because the name was wrong maybe it was not Ad Reinhardt who was dead. But all the statements was there to state it. Black monk of pix. Was cartoons in PM now defunct. The sorrows is true, the surmises is no evade. It is too true the sorrows. Reinhardt he dead. Don't say in the clips how he died, maybe just sat down and give up in front of the black picture. Impossible to believe.

Maybe if Reinhardt had the sense to die quietly in quietist studio it is becoming soon the long procession of big woes and he seen it come.

Maybe the sorrows is coming to roost and to lay the biggest egg you ever did see and he seen the sorrow coming with the egg to lay and he walked off into his picture.

Impossible to believe but is truth nevertheless too much sorrows.

How to grasp with the grapple sorrows? How to understand

the excellence of the great squares of black now done in? Glad he was to become the Jews exhibit this year for final success and laurels before the departure. He have this satisfaction how he was in Life think of the satisfaction probably so much it caused death. For to appear in Life is too often the cause of death.

Tomorrow the solemns. The requiems alone in the hermit hatch. Before the ikons the offering. The oblations. The clean oblations all round thunder quiet silence black picture oblations. Make Mass beautiful silence like big black picture speaking requiem. Tears in the shadows of hermit hatch requiems blue black tone. Sorrows for Ad in the oblation quiet peace request rest. Tomorrow is solemns in the hermit hatch for old lutheran reinhardt commie paintblack. Tomorrow is the eternal solemns fending off the purge-fire place non catch old skipper reinhardt safely by into the heavens. Tomorrow is the solemns and the barefoots and the ashes and the masses, oldstyle liturgy masses without the colonels and without the sargeants yelling sit down. Just old black quiet requiems in hermit hatch with decent sorrows good bye college chum.

It is all solemns and sads all over beginning to fade out people in process before comes the march of ogres and djinns. Well out of the way is safe Reinhardt in his simple black painting the final statement includes all.

Next thing you know the procession of weevils and the big germ. Pardon the Big Germ in capitals. It is now waking in the labor-blossoms a big pardon Big Germ. Ad is well out of sight in his blacks. It is likely too true the bad fortunes and the sorrows. Gypsy Rose Lee look in her crystal ball and see no more jokes and no more funnies it is not any more like thirty seven college chums. I must therefore cease and sit in the sorrows. I was not write before because I was in the dump with a sickness. Nothing bad. But you can only daid oncet. Like said uncle arthur in the aforesaid. Well is all silence in the den of glooms. Look around at some cheerful flower.

Lv.

Oh Chauncey,
 You are right. It is sorrows for old Reinhardt. One could weep
with out let for old Reinhardt. The clipping is fall to me from Rice.
I read it the last of many letters (offers of millions in every one). I
sit near the sea & almost fall into it from sorrow.
 & then I sit (as seldom enough we do) in a church & look at
the black & grey squares of the tiles, till the spirit is somewhat
mended.
 & then all through the whole dark night it is Reinhardt,
Reinhardt.
 (& ever since then.)
 not that it could have happened, just that it did.
 (&just that it's unthinkable world without him.)
 but there is no such world.
 one time at a party when a girl was reading palms, he showed
us his: his right was the mirror/image of the left. what he was
meant to be & what he became were exactly the same.
 (didn't surprise him much: crazy for symmetries.)
 well, it's into the symmetries for us all some day, & from now
on dobbin take the hindmost.
 Rice saw him about a week before then (looking thin, but ok);
he said he had painted one painting; now wanted to make one
movie & write one book.
 I'm glad you were there in the hermit-cell to say the right kind
of liturgy. I've been saying every wrong kind, since the sorrows
fell, but I think it will all be heard right.
 (everything will be heard right sometime.)
 No sargeants yelling sit down. is sergeants all over the
atmosphere. pressing right into the studiroom, sargeants &
weevils. & great woes hanging over every infant joy.
 better in the old days(1928), with drinks & a little melancholy,
than now with no drinks & great woes everywhere.
 & what is this about Gypsy Rose & the crystal ball? is a germ
in the crystal ball? Big Germ? a whole long procession of sorrows?
 then he was right to slip off into the painting, quiet as sam.
quietistic triumphant. samsum agronistes.

say us liturgies every one.
Lv,
Lax

Dear Rollo:

Well guess what it is Yom Kippur and I have elected to race the old race with the sun, that is to say the waiting race to see who goes first to supper, me or him. Well at five o'clock it became evident that Joshua had stopped the sun with the walls of Jericho and furthermore it was by that time sunset in New York, not to mention two a.m. in Israel and therefore I put on the Spanish rice to simmer and presently fell to, or fell in, with gusto, musto, presto and Django (four attendant sprites).

Now to the serious business of the momento. First is you know how Slate is dead. First Reinhardt and now Slates. One Saturday Slate goes to overwork some more in his Law office and gets the pains in the chest so the dr tells him go to the hospital for tests and while in the midst of the tests he over and died. Middle September old Slate he died. What with everybody roll over and die it makes a fellow think and begin to wonder. Poor old Slate he died. Mary Ann no more Slate I mean Mary Ellen. He was going to be coming here some more about the revision of the laws on account of my birthright (a mess of pottage). Too much law. I told him two years ago to lay off the law. It is too bad some fellows don't know when to quit.

Then on top of that Seymour he get in the hospital with the pains same only so far as I have heard he is not dead.

Well, and then some more on top of that I sent you a cablegram to say Slate was dead and what is my astonish when it comes back from the Vested Uniates that you was gone with no forwards address. This set me to thinking and mumbling within my beards more than ever because what is this I think you must be in the hoosegow for certain or maybe the victim of circumstances too numerous to mention. So then I think and think and I write finally to Gladio and she comes back with no you wasn't in the hoosegow but only on a state visit to Bosnia-Herzegovina. I am full

of relief heartfelt let us be careful not to lose any more of the
fellows because now is scarce the old friends.

My Gow scarce is the old friends and multiple the new
sorrows. Such sorrows as require two Yom Kippurs in the week.
Never saw such a dam bibful of sorrows. As each grows old so
grows multiple the sorrow. Evening sun go down with big curtain
of St. Louis blues. Morning come up in St James Infirmario. Great
is the laments. How is eating in the streets garbage for crocuses?
How is blinded the shiny gold? How is the Lamia whip out her
pap in the middle of ruins? Dolor hath a fine fat pup roaring in the
empty streets. It is a great business of howling in the archways
with hairy ones to dance over the locksteps of Babylums: proh
dolor, oy veh. Ululuat Propheta, indeed the prophet is all choked
from the hair in his teeth. Thus it is silent the prophet and loud the
parliament of owls and skrikes. Everything is logbound in a
milliondollar gnashing of teeth. I lie on the floor face down for
dilemmas and it is everywhere made the Bluemonday moan.

Enough I go to prepare the pencils of an Hieronymus Bosch.
Addio.

XXXVI. ROBERT LAX   *Kalimpest Oct 15 67*

Oh, alas, oh Merton,
            now indeed we are all undone; it is our undoing now,
everyone. with the passing of Dom John Slate is our generation all
dissolved, resolved. whatever is left gentle in the world, gone up
in a fume. we are only left (& in no shape, either) to tell each other
the story.

            how i am glad nevertheless that he came out to see you. (glad,
too, i went to see him & spend there the night, the day before i left
for greeks.) as to his passing, i have mourn his passing since the
first day i knew him: that anyone that rare should ever be obliged
to push along. yet now pushed has he.

            as to his rarity, let us in no way exaggerate his rarity: there has
been none like him in the histories before, nor likely to be in the
histories to come (saving only pico, whom we're not inclined to
save). not only his mind, but his humour; not only his humour but
his aforementioned gentleness, already mentioned in some former

scraps above.

i was in the belgrades when these catastrophes take place: slate among the deads; seymour in the hospital; your telegrams nonreaching; & soon after, Benji dies. my sister reft, & alone in her house. it is, as you tell her, a bad year for us all.

your comfort: that these are the good guys, & they checking out is comfort indeed. cogently stated. in fact, we are all checking out: ready, unready; willing, unwilling. (now blows the wind & every leaf's a skimmer.)

(i seen slate once in olean & him asleep with folded hands: he look even then like some welsh king or bishop on his sarcophashanks.)

write me sometime about his visits out there; & send me, if you can, a word of cheer from the woods.

Yrs,

Frank

XXXVII. THOMAS MERTON   *Oct 31, 1967*

Marse Joe:

Guess what marse here is woe's race. Here is Mose ways to tish vup. Here is most waste of teshuvah. It is the new inspirits. It is the concricks or comic cribs of the race. It is the next race the final fun, the olympic sidestep.

Here is the conscript pun. The running jug. The fleeting nig. Exacape from the fermeto grape. Not drink. Not tipplit. Teshuvip. Renuncio. Repeat. This is the conscropt race, the corncob place under the temples Drape.

There is here the rape of the clock. The washouts of tempo's million dollar stake. The warp of the investment.

Guess what marse here is woe's race to the post with a concraped poemast.

Here is Reds block at the gate with a compost.

Here is the fatal arts, the end of prevention.

Here is the jam of the nit nat, the phlegm of the ocean.

It is here the new poems I follow after with my conscript plovers my lightline flitting.

Have a mars bar of the new poperies.

Answer me this. When in the muds of a conscript proem you wish two big O 's like so I have draw with the poncif, one with no circumbrave and the other circumcised with a con-flex (box of nitty gritty rednut kellog for the breakers). Now I repeat when one wishes two O's must he explain for the prints? I presume there is an explain for the prints but I do not know the lingo. I write to Jonathan Williams.

How do you make the cornflex poem for the kellog prints? How do you deal with the business? Whom to consult? Whom to arraign? Who to bombard with the deseign? Whom to circumvent with the accents?

O the laments of old Slate. Was here with his laughing welsh in Mayo. Was drinking orange wine averred harmless and spoke welsh. Was insulting the provincials of Theleme and Barbasol college (home of my resident prints). He was here with a vast acceleration and laughs. He was here with a bow wow argument about the VN waw. We was in the Hawaiian temples with a Father and Miss Pat of the libraries and we was fight like catsup dogs over the VN waw and even all the waitresses and hired helps was joining in. I was nearly lynched and stabbed to death with forks though some was on my side. It is never a limit to the laments of Old Slates and Old Reinhardt. Truly the bloom has faded.

It is time to brush the dog and fling out the cat. And wash the coffee and drench the treat. And put away the muscraps and ampty the globbidge. There is always too ample the globbidge.

WESTERN FELLOW STUDENTS SALUTE
WITH CALYPSO ANTHEMS
THE MOVIE CAREER OF ROBERT LAX

". . . a personal poem sent to a friend who lives in Greece, a poet, who is not a movie star but who wrote me some obscure information about 'being in a movie.' This epic news occasioned the poem. I am still in the dark about the movie however."

We western fellow students salute with Calypso anthems
Your movie career in Greece oh famous Robert with your hat
Your sense of humor and your wry antics
Have made you notorious on the screens and TV's do not forget
It was your ancient association with Columbia U
That has placed you upon the top pinnacle where you are now at
Give sensitive response and grateful testimonies at ALMA MAT.

Now that you are a movie king and move with the elite
With that imposing *barba* contrasting with the white hat
Your sense of humor and your college capers for the screen public
Will appear like a vision in the eyes of the multitude
While you are portrayed in love with a stellar pulchritude
All for the visions of the less fortunate
Who lurk in the shadows of the cinema and view
(As once you did The Marx Brothers) who else but You?
This is principally (you must admit it) due
To the radical and wholesome influence of creative Columbia U
So astounding are you on the pinnacle of fame where you are now at
Do not forget your former fellow students nor your Alma Mat.

We on the other hand abiding on the distant progressive shore
Of our impressive continent hail more and more
The waving flag and the principle of might is right
Having little time for art and music, but only to create
New marvels of engineering and technology we are up to date
Though we may not appear in films or on the TV we tirelessly
     remain

In business offices and old folks homes and automats
We too are a modest credit to Alma Mat.

I most of all with consummate fellow feeling and warm religious
    glow congratulate
Your religious witness and achievement for the Cat-
lick Church among the Greek Orthodox with the black hat
You are besides being a poet and a well known wit
Doing in your own inimitable way your ecumenical bit
Thus as for the Greek film you fail to dodge the custard pie
You retain a glint of hesychasm in your eye
To show the Orthos that you know where you are at
You are on the very summit of Mount Ararat
Thinking at once of Noah and of Alma Mat.

Thus in a kindred spirit of faith and pat-
riotism I climb my religious dolmen and raise the stupendous flag
I salute you where I wrestle on the ascetic mat
I fling ashes in the air over my greying eremitical head
I holler at the other dervishes and beat my pet cat
All in the name of fellowship and the right hand
Proffered in communion to every living man woman and child

Regardless of color creed or ugly face
I am in a condition of ecstasy over the human race
In whose history this important and significant date
Will surely substitute universal love for universal hate
The weapon will drop from the hand and the hand will stretch out
In friendship while a smile untwists the distorted mout'
Your film will surely make for camaraderie between mouse and cat
Provided only you are respectful and not oblivious of Alma Mat.

by Thomas Merton [1967]

from: *The Collected Poems of Thomas Merton*
N. Y., New Directions. 1977, pp. 811-814.